THE DECISION TO VOLUNTEER

Why people give their time and how you can engage them

BETH GAZLEY, PH.D. AND MONICA DIGNAM

RESEARCH AND ANALYSIS FROM ASAE & THE CENTER FOR ASSOCIATION LEADERSHIP

The follow-up to *The Decision to Join:* New research into the voluntary contributions and motivations of **26,305** association members

asae & the center™
for association leadership

WASHINGTON, D.C.

ASAE & The Center for Association Leadership
1575 I Street, NW
Washington, DC 20005-1103
Phone: 202-371-0940 (when calling from within the Washington, D.C. metropolitan area)
Phone: 888-950-2723 (when calling from outside the Washington, D.C. metropolitan area)
Fax: 202-220-6439
Email: books@asaecenter.org

ASAE & The Center for Association Leadership connect great ideas to great people to inspire leadership and achievement within the association community.

John H. Graham IV, CAE, President and CEO, ASAE
Susan Robertson, CAE, Senior Vice President, ASAE & The Center for Association Leadership
Monica Dignam, Vice President, Industry & Market Research, ASAE & The Center for Association Leadership
Clare Inzeo, Research Associate, Industry & Market Research, ASAE & The Center for Association Leadership
Keith C. Skillman, CAE, Vice President, Publications, ASAE & The Center for Association Leadership
Baron Williams, CAE, Director, Book Publishing, ASAE & The Center for Association Leadership

A complete catalog of ASAE titles is available on the Web at www.asaecenter.org/bookstore.

Cover design by Beth Lower
Interior design by Cimarron Design, cimarrondesign.com
International Standard Book Number, 10 digit: 0-88034-299-4
International Standard Book Number, 13 digit: 978-0-88034-299-5

Printed in the United States of America.

10 9 8 7 6 5 4 3 2 1

Table of Contents

Table of Exhibits

Acknowledgements

I N THE TRUEST SPIRIT of association, THE DECISION TO VOLUNTEER has been a collaborative effort, involving many for the good of the order. ASAE & The Center for Association Leadership Industry Research prepared the study, working extensively with numerous volunteers and staff. We are ever-grateful to all those who contributed their expertise in support of this study. ASAE & The Center for Association Leadership extend a special thanks to the following individuals and organizations:

Cosponsors

- American Association of Orthodontists
- American College of Healthcare Executives
- American Heart Association National Center
- American Industrial Hygiene Association
- American Institute of CPAs
- American Massage Therapy Association
- American Nurses Association
- American Society for Quality
- American Society of Civil Engineers
- American Society of Heating, Refrigerating and Air-Conditioning Engineers
- American Society of Mechanical Engineers
- American Society of Plastic Surgeons
- American Speech-Language-Hearing Association
- AORN Association of periOperative Registered Nurses
- Illinois Education Association
- Institute of Electrical & Electronics Engineers
- NACE International
- National Association of Secondary School Principals
- National Funeral Directors Association
- Oncology Nursing Society
- Project Management Institute
- School Nutrition Association
- Society of Petroleum Engineers

Volunteers

We thank the ASAE & The Center for Association Leadership Component Relations Section Council, and particularly 2007–2008 council Chair Peggy M. Hoffman, council members Linda S. Chreno, CAE, Kimberly Fischer, CAE, KiKi L'Italien, and Leslie T. White, ARM, CIC, CPCU, CRM, and Membership Section Council member Stuart K. Meyer for their work in preparing the "Acting on the Findings" section provided at the end of Chapters 3–7.

And, as always, we express our most sincere appreciation to the association executives and staff who supported this study.

We welcome any comments about the study. Please address comments to ASAE's Industry & Market Research Department at **evaluations@asaecenter.org**.

CHAPTER 1

What Frames the Decision to Volunteer?

T HE IMMENSE VALUE OF volunteerism to a healthy civic life can hardly be disputed. Volunteers allow both public and nonprofit organizations to expand their reach well beyond the capacity of paid staff. Volunteers bring new energy and expertise, and the credibility of a job performed without an expectation of pay. They offer representation from diverse constituencies. Within professional associations, volunteers are essential as the field experts who ensure the credibility and quality of educational and certification programs. Volunteers actively recruit new members and mentor and support young professionals. And volunteers fill an essential governance role as trustees and committee members.

Despite the strategic importance of volunteers, there is still much we do not know about the volunteers who serve membership organizations. In the nonprofit universe, charities have enjoyed most of the research attention, especially when it comes to volunteer management. A gap exists in the research on mutual-benefit associations in particular and on professional and workplace volunteering in general. This book helps to fill that gap, using the largest and most comprehensive survey to date of association members and their volunteering behavior.

Who is This Study For?

The principal audience for this book is the association or nonprofit professional charged with volunteer management. However, in most associations and nonprofit organizations, all programmatic staff have some regular interaction with volunteers. Because volunteers are so sensitive to the messages they receive from staff, we hope that the results of this study will be shared widely. You will find it useful to discuss our key findings with staff as you engage in strategic planning that depends on volunteer resources. Board and committee members will benefit from our discussion of the board's role in establishing the priorities and strategic objectives of a volunteer program, since this effort drives so many other considerations related to the volunteer program, including budget. And membership services staff will benefit from the ability to understand how member satisfaction might improve by increasing affiliation through volunteer involvement.

Organization of This Book

THE DECISION TO VOLUNTEER offers a comprehensive examination of the volunteering behavior of association members. The study behind the book was designed as a comparative examination of association volunteering—to understand workplace and professional volunteering in the context of a member's other civic activities (such as community volunteering) and in the context of his or her personal and professional and family situation. This approach gives us information about the volunteering background of association members and also helps us understand what priority they give to association service when they volunteer elsewhere. In an internet survey fielded in November–December 2007, we asked a random sample of members from 23 cosponsoring organizations more than 30 questions, covering the following topics:

- Where do they perform their community volunteering?
- Where do they perform their association (professional) volunteering?
- How were they recruited, and what do they do?
- What motivates them to volunteer?
- If they do not volunteer, why not?
- What would encourage them to volunteer in the future?

Of the 185,975 individuals we surveyed, 26,305 responded. We then combined their responses with demographic information—their ages, family situations, career status, locations, and membership history—and organized the book around the way that some of these personal characteristics can influence association volunteer activity. For example, how might the career level or employment status of an association member influence the activities to which he or she is drawn? What is the demographic profile of the most active volunteers? Can we count on those who are active in their communities to volunteer for their professional associations as well? Is there a difference between men and women in what they choose to do? And how might family and professional responsibilities influence your members' capacity to support associations as volunteers?

In this book, you will find answers to these and many other questions. Besides its wealth of data, the book's value is enhanced further by its emphasis on *application*—on a thorough discussion of how the findings translate into management steps that you might consider to strengthen your volunteer programs. Wherever possible, we draw on the best in volunteerism scholarship and association management literature to help you understand how to make use of this information to recruit and retain volunteers more effectively.

Key Findings

The study and its analysis yielded numerous key findings, among them the following:

- **Association members are highly engaged people.** On average, the individuals who participated in this study volunteer more than national levels and for more organizations. They represent an ideal demographic group for volunteer recruitment generally. But they reserve most of their volunteer hours for community organizations, not for associations. Turnover among association volunteers is high. These are busy people with many competing opportunities to volunteer. Associations will have to work hard to get their attention.

- **Values drive volunteer choices.** In studies of volunteerism, the most commonly cited reason for serving has been a desire to help others and to create a better society. We found in this study that the same holds true for professional volunteering. While association members still expect career benefits from their professional volunteering, they are also interested in volunteering for reasons bigger than themselves, especially to build a stronger profession.

- **The power of the direct ask.** The top methods by which members were recruited into volunteer activities were through participation in chapters or annual meetings, and through a request by staff or other volunteers. Passive recruitment techniques such as web site postings were not nearly as effective as more direct approaches. Like donors, volunteers respond best when approached directly with meaningful tasks.

- **A meaningful experience keeps them coming back.** Once you get them, how do you keep them? As busy professionals, association volunteers are no different from most community volunteers in expecting a chance to work with like-minded people, network, keep skills sharp or learn a new skill, pass on their knowledge, and contribute to a cause they believe in. Above all, people who volunteer for associations expect to be involved effectively. In our demographic analyses, we also learned that volunteer expectations vary according to where members are in their careers. One size will not fit all, and associations must design flexible and multiple volunteer activities for their members.

- **Involving the younger generations.** Nationally, some policymakers have expressed a concern about the volunteer supply, suggesting that younger citizens are not willing to fill the gap left by retiring older volunteers. We found little evidence of this trend in our study. Although the Millennial and Gen X members were slightly less engaged than older members, and are likely to volunteer differently, they actually believe more strongly in the importance of volunteering. The challenge for associations will be in finding meaningful and substantive ways to involve these less experienced but eager young professionals. Given the high turnover rates we found among association volunteers, the effort to recruit new volunteers, particularly from among the youngest members, is critical.

- **The professional benefits of volunteerism.** Two thirds of our survey respondents said they look for opportunities to connect volunteering to their professional work. Most were happy with their association volunteer work. We found a strong connection between the number of hours they volunteered and their satisfaction with professional volunteering. In fact, many regard volunteering as a benefit of membership; they see the association volunteer work they have done as something that has made them better professionals. This is a powerful message that associations can use in both member and volunteer recruitment strategies.

- **Recognizing the "ad hoc" volunteer.** When we think about association volunteers, the first people who might come to mind are those who fill board and committee seats. Our study suggests that most association volunteers are performing low-profile services such as mentoring, membership recruitment, technical writing, or activities that might be further off the radar screen for association staff. The risk is in assuming that these ad hoc volunteers require less attention. Rather, we suggest that staff and board members find ways to identify, support, and acknowledge all volunteer contributions.

- **Organizational strategies can support or discourage volunteering.** We found that family, work, and geography can all limit volunteer participation. But members told us that many of the reasons they did not volunteer for their professional association are within the organization's power to address. In fact, the number one reason they did not volunteer was a lack of information about the opportunities. Other addressable issues we encountered in our study included poor follow-through with volunteers, forgetting to thank them, poor communication, lack of support or training, unclear roles, and high transportation expenses. In this book, we talk further about how an understanding of the essential elements of a volunteer program can increase participation among your members, beginning with a clear understanding among board and staff about the strategic value of volunteers.

Making This Study Work for You

We believe that the effort to engage your members as volunteers can produce multiple benefits for your organization beyond the obvious benefit of their labor. Associations that succeed at effective volunteer involvement may have a unique opportunity, not generally open to community organizations, to engage volunteers in a more permanent way. As we see it, in their personal lives, people volunteer according to their time in life—for school activities when they are young, for family activities when they are parenting. That means that their volunteer interests change over time.

Associations have an enormous advantage here in that people don't change their professions as often as they change other life events. Professions for most people last a lifetime, and many people make long-term commitments to the association that serves their professional niche. This commitment can extend even beyond retirement. Much like paid work, association volunteer work can have a career path, where opportunities parallel a volunteer's experience, interests, and seniority. Associations that understand how to turn volunteer work into a long-term and mutually beneficial experience are likely to reap the rewards not only in expanded services but in more satisfied members.

This study presents the aggregate findings of a survey of members associated with 23 diverse associations. Since your own volunteers will be as diverse as your particular membership base, the first step in understanding how to recruit, engage, and keep *your* volunteers is getting to know them. We hope that associations will receive a great deal of practical wisdom from this book alone, but we also hope that many of you will take the next step in surveying your own volunteers. This book includes some recommended approaches for producing the information about your volunteers that will support an effective volunteer management program. Each chapter concludes with some practical suggestions for how association professionals can apply the information to their own organizations. These suggestions, offered by an experienced group of volunteer managers, will prove invaluable to applying the results to the real-world challenges faced by association professionals on a daily basis. Effective volunteer management, like any program, requires a serious investment of expertise and resources. We hope you find this book useful in building a strong volunteer program in your organization.

CHAPTER 2

The Study Framework

I N *BY THE PEOPLE,* a historical account of voluntary activity in the United States, Ellis and Campbell (2005) observe that volunteering is often misunderstood. They note, for example, the tendency for observers to assume that volunteers represent only select segments of the population and that voluntary activity occurs only for charitable reasons and not for other purposes. One result of this assumption about volunteers is that most past studies of volunteering have focused only on volunteering for charitable organizations. And a methodological limitation of present national studies of volunteering is that they are addressed at individuals who volunteer and do not tell us much about the organizations where volunteer labor is directed.

As a result, we do not know how much volunteering is directed at mutual-benefit organizations and nonprofits other than charitable organizations. But we do know that the 23 cosponsoring organizations all joined this study because they have volunteers they wish to understand better. If your organization is in a similar situation, you will gain much useful information from this study about who your volunteers are, what they contribute, and what they expect from their service. In fact, this study addresses the needs of all associations because by law, every nonprofit organization, regardless of its tax status, must have at least one director or trustee, who almost always is unpaid. In short, because every nonprofit organization involves some volunteers, effective volunteer recruitment, support, and retention are important to all member-serving organizations.

This chapter provides an overview of voluntary activity in the United States and of volunteer management in the context of association management. Further, we discuss general theories behind voluntary behavior to explain what motivates individuals to donate their time and labor to professional organizations and elsewhere. Subsequent chapters report on our findings.

Volunteering in the United States

Of the estimated 1.4 million nonprofit organizations in the United States, charities and foundations make up two thirds of the total, and noncharitable social welfare and mutual-benefit organizations represent the rest (NCNA 2006). Volunteers serve as essential resources in many of these organizations. Aside from the board members who serve nonprofit organizations, an estimated three quarters of all nonprofits also involve volunteers in direct service and other activities.

> *Aside from the board members who serve nonprofit organizations, an estimated three quarters of all nonprofits also involve volunteers in direct service and other activities.*

A common myth about volunteering is that it is "nice but not necessary" and perhaps "more hindrance than help"—in other words, volunteers provide an added value to society, but society would operate just as well without them. Like most myths, there is a grain of truth to this perspective in that some highly professionalized organizations depend only minimally on volunteers. However, in the words of the Corporation for National and Community Service (2008), a federal agency charged with promoting volunteerism in the United States, "volunteering is no longer just nice to do. It is a necessary aspect of meeting the most pressing needs facing our nation: crime, gangs, poverty, disasters, illiteracy, and homelessness. It is also an important part of maintaining the health of our citizens, as research consistently shows that those who volunteer, especially those 65 years and older, lead healthier lives than those who do not engage in their communities."

In addition to the benefits that they accrue personally, volunteers add substantial economic value to American life. Volunteers provide an estimated $240 billion annually in unpaid labor. Gifts of time and money are closely related, meaning that most volunteers make philanthropic contributions in addition to the gift of their time. In 2006, individuals within the United States contributed $223 billion in charitable gifts alone (Center on Philanthropy 2007). Finally, neither of these figures accounts for the long-term impact that volunteer labor makes when it helps to educate citizens, prevent crime, improve public health, and make other contributions to the quality of civic life. Altogether, the public value that volunteers create through their labor, expertise, gifts, and example is profound and difficult to capture through numbers alone.

Volunteering Trends and Patterns

One in Four Americans Volunteers Through an Organization

The percentage of Americans who report that they volunteer has varied widely according to the surveying methods employed (Brudney and Gazley 2006). Figures range from approximately one quarter to one half of all Americans, depending on question wording, sampling methods, and the kind of volunteering captured in the study. Part of the difficulty in measuring volunteer behavior is in the ambiguity of the term itself, since *volunteering* means different things to different people (Ellis and Campbell 2005). Most researchers find it easier and more accurate to capture only the "formal" or institutional volunteering that individuals perform (since people perform their service *for* an organization, they can more readily identify this activity as volunteering). We follow this common practice in our study of association volunteering since this study also focuses on institutional volunteering. But we acknowledge that people also serve their communities through additional, ad-hoc activities known as "informal" volunteerism—such as helping a neighbor or family member or helping out at a school or sporting event (Weitzman et al. 2002).

At present, the two sources of data on volunteering considered to be most methodologically sound are the Bureau of Labor Statistics (BLS) Current Population Survey, a biennial government sample of the U.S. labor force, and the Indiana University Center on Philanthropy's Panel Study

(COPPS), a longitudinal survey of charitable behavior in 7,400 U.S. households. The BLS data—the most current and hence the comparison point for the ASAE & The Center for Association Leadership study—show that in 2007, in 26 percent of American households, at least one adult volunteered to or through an organization (BLS 2008). This represents more than 61 million individuals performing unpaid service for public and private sector organizations.

By contrast, 86 percent of the 26,305 association members who answered our survey are volunteering for their associations or elsewhere. So it is important to bear in mind from the outset that our study is different from national studies of volunteering behavior and comparable to them only in a limited way. Our survey was answered mostly by volunteers and was fielded only to people who are members of an association—a demographically unrepresentative sample of professionals. As a result, its value principally is in understanding volunteer behavior among association members who volunteer and, to a lesser extent, understanding why they do not volunteer.

The Demographics of Volunteering

When we fielded this survey, we found that a few respondents questioned our inclusion of questions about personal characteristics such as gender, age, and family characteristics. What can questions of such a personal nature have to do with volunteering, we were asked? In fact, these questions are essential to understanding volunteering behavior. Personal background matters because people are socialized into volunteering largely through family activities (and, to a lesser extent, professional activities). Children who grew up in households in which parents volunteered are more likely to volunteer themselves. Men and women have different volunteer patterns when they assume different roles within a family unit with respect to civic activity. Marital and socioeconomic status matter because financial stability enables people to engage in volunteer activities more easily. Country of citizenship matters because social and professional expectations vary around the globe, along with the legal frameworks that protect civic activity.

The following information, based on various sources such as the BLS, provides a snapshot of the American volunteer. Volunteer characteristics

Additional information about volunteering in the U.S. and around the globe can be obtained from these sources:
- Bureau of Labor Statistics Current Population Survey at **www.bls.gov/cps**
- Canadian Survey of Giving, Volunteering and Participating at **www.givingandvolunteering.ca**
- Center for Civil Society Studies, Johns Hopkins University at **www.jhu.edu/ccss**
- Centre Européen du Volontariat / European Volunteer Centre at **www.cev.be**
- Corporation for National and Community Service at **www.cns.gov**
- Indiana University Center on Philanthropy at **www.philanthropy.iupui.edu/research**
- Points of Light and Hands On Network at **www.handsonnetwork.org**

vary considerably from country to country, along with the extent of research efforts to understand voluntary activity. Since our study involves U.S.-based organizations and the respondents principally are U.S. citizens, this snapshot reflects what we understand about American volunteers. For further information about volunteering in other countries, as well as the United States, consider using the resources provided in the box.

Within the United States, the demographic profile of the American volunteer is fairly stable. Women volunteer slightly more than men, married people substantially more than those who are single, parents with children under age 18 more than those without, and the employed more than the unemployed (BLS 2008). Overall, socio-economic status and education are the strongest predictors of formal volunteering, less so for informal volunteering. Volunteerism is also strongly linked to other kinds of civic engagement. Volunteers are more likely to vote, engage in political organizing, and make charitable gifts when compared to non-volunteers (Kutner and Love 2003; Weitzman et al. 2002).

As Exhibit 2.1 illustrates, the level of volunteer involvement among Americans follows an S-curve, where teenagers are more likely to volunteer than adults in their twenties, but individuals aged 35–44 are most likely to volunteer, followed by older age groups (BLS 2008). Generally, more individuals volunteer at midlife than at younger or older ages, with the exception of teenagers, who are increasingly engaged in volunteering.

EXHIBIT 2.1

2007 U.S. Rates of Volunteering by Age Group

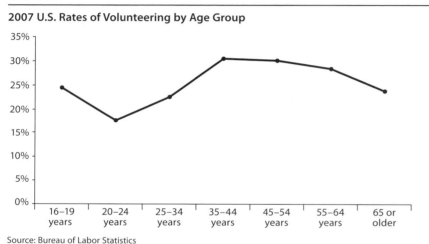

Source: Bureau of Labor Statistics

Racial and cultural comparisons are more difficult to make in studies of giving and volunteering. Although some sources, including the BLS, suggest that White non-Hispanic Americans engage in formal volunteering more than Blacks, Hispanics, or Asians, racial differences are reduced substantially when informal volunteering is included and when education and socio-economic status are held equal. Traditional survey questions may not accurately capture volunteering by ethnic minorities or distinctions within minority categories (Kutner and Love 2003). Some observers also note a weaker community effort to involve minority groups in volunteering, which in turn might lead to less measurable voluntary activity (Weitzman et al. 2002). In other words, racial and cultural patterns may influence not only the frequency but the nature of voluntary activity.

Volunteers contribute an average of 52 hours per year to organizations, or one hour per week. The amount of donated hours doubles to 96 hours per year for volunteers ages 65 and older. This figure is quite stable across age and gender groups, and an increase in socio-economic status does not lead to more donated hours (BLS 2008).

The scope and focus of volunteer efforts depends considerably on the family status and age of the volunteer. The number of hours volunteered is influenced by the numbers and ages of children in a household. While having young children tends to limit available time for volunteering, adult volunteers with school-age children tend to volunteer more frequently, often for activities involving their children. In national studies, nearly half of those adults with children under 18 volunteer for educational institutions, sports leagues, scouting, or other youth-related causes, while those without children volunteer more often for civic, environmental, religious, and community service organizations.

In addition to these family-related activities, on average, 5 percent of Americans volunteer for civic, political, professional, or international organizations (BLS 2008). And about one quarter of all volunteers support public agencies at the federal, state, and local levels (Weitzman et al. 2002). Most Americans focus their volunteer energies on only one organization: 69 percent volunteered for one organization, 27 percent volunteered for two or three, and 4 percent volunteered for four or more organizations during 2007. The most frequent kinds of activity overall are fundraising (10.9 percent) and tutoring (10.8 percent), followed by collecting or distributing food (9.2 percent); general labor (8.3 percent); professional assistance, including board and committee service (7.6 percent); and sports coaching (5.8 percent).

Rates of Volunteering Are Stable, but the Patterns Have Changed

Past and present studies have observed relatively small increases over time in the percentage of Americans who volunteer (BLS 2008; Toppe, Kirsch, and Michel 2002; Weitzman et al. 2002). The stability in volunteering trends surprises some observers, since policymakers, schools, and philanthropic organizations have increased their emphasis over time on civic engagement (Brudney and Gazley 2006). In some limited instances, we do see portions of the population increasing their level of civic engagement; this trend is most visible with individuals of high school and college age, who are exposed in school to an increasing number of civic engagement and service-learning activities. We also see an increasing emphasis on volunteer promotion among the Baby Boomers: they represent an important age group for voluntary activity, to the extent that the White House, AARP, and other organizations have engaged in a coordinated effort to encourage them to continue volunteering post-retirement so as not to lose their valuable contributions (Independent Sector 2003; Kutner and Love 2003; Lindblom 2001).

Other changes appear principally in patterns of volunteer behavior. Many of the patterns are associated with changes in the American labor force. For example, the addition of large numbers of women to the workforce in the past two generations has reduced their relative level of participation in volunteering and narrowed the margin of difference between men and women. Some new patterns have arisen out of technological opportunities: the increase in cross-national volunteering is supported by the relative ease of international travel, while an increase in internet-based or "virtual volunteering" follows the development of a global internet system (Murray and Harrison 2005; Smith, Ellis and Brewis 2005).

Some patterns offer new recruiting opportunities for the volunteer manager. Americans report that they volunteer increasingly through workplace opportunities. One quarter of those who volunteer through the workplace do so alongside their coworkers (Kutner and Love 2003; Weitzman et al. 2002). One quarter of all volunteers learned about the opportunity through their workplace or employer (Toppe, Kirsch, and Michel 2002). To tap this new and valuable source of voluntary labor, civic and charitable organizations are working more closely with employers to promote workplace volunteering. Many of the nation's largest employers now offer incentives to employees who volunteer. As a result, volunteering that is related to a profession is viewed increasingly by employers and colleagues as a virtue rather than a detriment to their professional responsibilities. Since our survey was aimed at many individuals who perform workplace volunteering for membership associations, this increasingly supportive organizational atmosphere is important to note.

> **Volunteering that is related to a profession is viewed increasingly by employers and colleagues as a virtue rather than a detriment to their professional responsibilities.**

Not all of these patterns are beneficial, however. Some create new recruitment and retention challenges for organizations. Although workplace volunteering is producing many new volunteers, a decreasing number of volunteers make a long-term commitment. Many more Americans now volunteer through short-term assignments such as those provided through "Days of Service" and corporate community projects. Short-term work assignments have grown to where they involve about the same number of volunteers as those who donate services through more traditional, year-round schedules (Kirsch, Hume, and Jalandoni 2000; Kutner and Love 2003). Over time, the number of hours donated per individual has decreased from about four hours per week one generation ago to an average of one hour per week in recent studies (BLS 2008; Weitzman et al. 2002). This type of short-term or "episodic" volunteer is considered harder to retain. In addition, from a cost-benefit perspective, host organizations that invest in volunteer management tools such as training must spend more on volunteers as turnover increases. However, since the "episodic" pattern in volunteering may be consistent with a general trend toward more individualistic and self-directed perspectives on work and leisure activities, this type of volunteering is likely here to stay among a large portion of adult Americans (Macduff 2005).

These patterns also suggest that while new volunteer opportunities arise as technology eases the barriers to volunteer involvement, a good portion of Americans remain under-involved in formal, long-term volunteering. Despite the best efforts of many national initiatives, three in four adult Americans do not volunteer. While this under-involvement occurs among all age groups, policymakers and service providers are particularly concerned about how these patterns of involvement will influence voluntary activity among a large and aging population of Baby Boomers as they approach retirement and about their ability to shape messages and programs that will engage this group (Center for Health Communication 2004; Eisner 2005). Practitioners are also interested in attracting younger volunteers to replace older volunteers as they become too frail to participate. The reasons why association members do not volunteer therefore became one of this study's points of interest.

Understanding Voluntary Behavior

Why Volunteer?

In past studies of those who volunteer, the most commonly cited reason for serving has been a desire to help others and create a better society. Volunteers also serve out of a sense of personal responsibility or civic duty, a desire to make a difference, and an extension of religious and spiritual convictions. They may also serve to pursue a personal interest in the cause or issue, out of a need for affiliation or desire to learn new skills, a desire for a new challenge, and to meet new people. They may volunteer to return good fortune, to continue a family tradition, and to fill up empty time (Brudney 2005; Cnaan and Goldberg-Glen 1991; Okun, Barr, and Herzog 1998; Prisuta 2003; Weitzman et al. 2002).

This list reflects the multitude of reasons that people provide for volunteering. As mentioned earlier, voluntary behavior is subject to a few myths and misassumptions. A persistent myth is that volunteers participate spontaneously in response to appeals for help from organizations that need their help. Another is that people volunteer purely for altruistic reasons.

Such perspectives overlook important facts about volunteering. First, volunteering is a calculated decision that is rarely spontaneous. Volunteers "may deliberate for considerable amounts of time about whether to volunteer, the extent of [their] involvement, and the degree to which particular activities [match their] own personal needs" (Clary et al. 1998, page 1517).

Secondly, not all voluntary activities can be linked to altruistic motivations. A volunteer who serves for "involuntary" reasons such as a legal or professional obligation (for example, a student who volunteers for course credit) clearly is motivated by more complicated factors. An individual who coaches her child's team and a group of citizens who clean up their own neighborhood both operate to improve their own quality of life (Burns et al. 2008). Likewise, an individual who performs services that build his or her own profession also intends to benefit from the outcomes.

The important point here is that volunteers contribute their time for both altruistic (other-serving) and instrumental (self-serving) reasons (McCurley and Lynch 1996). In fact, rather than choosing between other-serving and self-serving goals, volunteers tend to express these two motivations simultaneously (Brudney 2005; Okun, Barr, and Herzog 1998). Thus, the most sophisticated studies into volunteer motivations have attempted to understand volunteer behavior as something more complicated than pure altruism. Scholars have built multi-dimensional models to understand the various drivers of voluntary activity. These models also help practitioners understand the motivations of particular age groups and professions. With career-related volunteering, for example, younger age groups may express more interest in using volunteering for career development. Older adults also manifest work-related interests but of a different kind: They may be more interested in staying active, feeling competent and useful, keeping existing skills sharp, passing on their knowledge, and maintaining social or business ties (Kutner and Love 2003; Okun, Barr, and Herzog 1998).

Because volunteer motivations are mixed, volunteerism is best viewed as a pro-social rather than a self-sacrificial activity; it benefits others but does not restrict the volunteer's own possible benefits (Brudney 1990). This is a useful connection to be made by professional and mutual-benefit organizations, where the public or social benefit of the voluntary activity may be less evident or non-existent when compared to professional benefits. In fact, from the volunteer's perspective, it may not matter.

For every volunteering adult American, two more who do not currently volunteer say that they would if given the right opportunity.

As for non-volunteers, there is strong social pressure on individuals to volunteer in the United States. This makes cross-national comparisons difficult and also makes it difficult to capture accurate data on why individuals might *not* volunteer. According to various surveys, non-volunteers most frequently report a lack of time as a barrier to involvement. Volunteers with children or adult dependents frequently cite competing family responsibilities. Seniors most often cite poor health but also lack of transportation (BLS 2004). Surveys also capture a small but persistent number of individuals who state that they were simply never asked to volunteer but would consider volunteering if they were approached by someone (Weitzman et al. 2002). In fact, studies find that for every volunteering adult American, two more who do not currently volunteer say that they would if given the right opportunity (BLS 2004).

Recruiting and Retaining Volunteers

Since volunteers serve for complex reasons, it is risky to assume that a volunteer serves without an expectation of reciprocal benefits of some kind (such as experience, connections, recognition). Your organization, whether charitable or non-charitable, will proceed best with an understanding that both your needs and the needs and expectations of the volunteer must be met for best results. In fact, another myth about volunteerism is that volunteers are "free" resources. Such a perspective does not take into account the commitment of staff time and other organizational resources that are required to make a volunteer program effective. Volunteer retention is further complicated by the fact that volunteers' motivations can evolve: A volunteer can enter service for altruistic reasons (e.g., desire to make a difference) but stay because of the personal benefits he or she derives from the activity (e.g., forging new social bonds) (Brudney 2005).

Organizations that regularly involve and depend on their volunteers must have a fairly sophisticated understanding of the management approaches that support volunteer involvement. Without an investment in their volunteer program, they risk volunteer churn, or refilling positions over and over as their volunteers move on to more satisfying opportunities. Few organizations calculate the costs of volunteer turnover even when they do the same for staff. Volunteer turnover tends to be substantially higher than turnover for paid staff. About one in three volunteers leaves his or her position on an annual basis, 10 times the turnover rate of paid nonprofit staff (at 3.1 percent) (Corporation for National and Community Service 2007; Gazley 2008). Higher turnover is to be expected given the unpaid nature of volunteer work. Nonetheless, ineffective or nonexistent volunteer management also contributes to turnover and can be addressed.

Meeting the Psychological Contract in Volunteering

Viewed another way, volunteers engage with an organization with an expectation of a certain experience. In human resources management, the concept of a psychological contract—a set of mutual expectations—has been applied to the employer-employee relationship. From an employers' perspective, important elements of the psychological contract might include an expectation of loyalty, a minimum length of stay, or a willingness to accept transfers. Employees might expect advancement, merit pay, training, and job security (Farmer and Fedor 1999; Rousseau 1995). Normally, these expectations would be formalized through a contract.

Volunteers also forge an informal psychological contract—an understanding that their service will generate some anticipated outcome—with the organization they serve. They anticipate benefits for a cause they support, an increase in the quality of their profession, a new experience, social opportunities, or access to training or other resources. The organization, in turn, might expect hard work, a certain length of service, or an imposed attendance standard. Since organizations usually offer their volunteers few tangible forms of remuneration, a volunteer must feel that his or her services are recognized and valued and that the organization cares about his or her well-being to believe the contract has been met. Organizations can capture this information about their volunteers through surveys, interviews, or observation, and those that do are in the best position to meet expectations and turn short-term volunteers into long-term resources.

When the psychological contract is broken, a volunteer is more apt to underperform or to leave. Not all reasons for a departure are within the control of the organization, but perhaps more reasons are controllable than are generally assumed. Following are some of the controllable reasons that volunteers leave. By *control* we mean that an organization has the ability, assuming resources and priorities agree, to meet these needs. Controllable reasons for which volunteers might leave include lack of transportation, ineffective interpersonal communication, acceptance problems between volunteers and paid staff or clients, unrealistic expectations on either the organization's or volunteer's part, unclear roles, inadequate training, underuse, overuse, conflicts of interest, and burnout. Uncontrollable reasons might include a physical move, return to work or school, health problems, or change in income or family responsibilities.

Effective Volunteer Management Tools

Why is the list of controllable reasons that volunteers leave so much longer than the list of uncontrollable reasons? Many studies have concluded that a good number of organizations do not have all of the volunteer management tools in place that they need. For example, they may train their volunteers but overlook the importance of training staff in how to work with volunteers. In a 2003 survey by the Urban Institute, fewer than half of U.S. charities reported that they incorporated any of the following volunteer management practices "to a large degree":

- Written job descriptions for volunteers
- Screening procedures to identify suitable volunteers
- Record keeping on volunteer hours and numbers
- Liability coverage or insurance protection for volunteers
- Recognition activities or ceremonies, training and professional development
- Annual measurement of the impact of volunteers (Hager and Brudney 2004).

Yet each of these activities is considered helpful in supporting volunteer retention. Matching volunteers to tasks can be particularly important, since volunteers arrive with quite varied skills and expectations. A common complaint from volunteers is that they are not given sufficiently challenging tasks (Hager and Brudney 2004; Jamison 2003). According to the Corporation for National and Community Service (2008), "volunteers will not continue to serve at an organization if they are not effectively managed. Indeed, recent studies show a disturbingly high level of volunteer turnover, making retention and an investment in effective management techniques that much more critical."

Hager and Brudney (2004) find a positive correlation between the amount of organizational investment in these various volunteer management tools and the perceived benefit that these organizations derive from voluntary activity. In other words, the extent to which organizations depend on volunteers may drive their investment in a volunteer program, and this in turn may increase the value of the return that they receive from volunteers.

EXHIBIT 2.2

The Volunteer Benefits/Volunteer Management Feedback Loop

Perceived benefits from volunteers   Investments in volunteer management

Source: Hager and Brudney 2004.

To summarize this review of the literature on volunteerism, we distill several important points:

- About one in four Americans volunteers, a figure that has increased only slightly over time.
- The strongest predictors of volunteerism are socio-economic status, gender, age, and family situation.
- Organizations have not tapped all of the volunteer resources that are available to them.
- Those who do volunteer have multiple reasons for doing so: Both altruism and personal or professional benefits play a role.
- Because volunteer motivations are mixed, volunteerism is best viewed as a pro-social rather than a self-sacrificial activity—it benefits others but does not restrict the volunteer's own possible benefits.
- Organizations could increase volunteer retention and reduce turnover by investing in volunteer management practices.

The Volunteer Functions Inventory

One of the tools that we employed to understand volunteer behavior within associations was the Volunteer Functions Inventory (VFI), developed by Gil Clary, Mark Snyder, and colleagues (1996; 1998; 1999). The VFI provides a window into a volunteer's take on the psychological contract by testing a volunteer's response to a series of scaled questions that gets at the multiple motives behind volunteering. According to its authors, all individuals volunteer for some combination of the following reasons, expressed as the personal and social functions or needs that volunteering serves:

- Values—to express or act on important values like humanitarianism
- Understanding—to learn more about the world or exercise skills that are unused
- Enhancement—to grow and develop psychologically
- Career—to gain career-related experience
- Social—to strengthen social relationships
- Protective—to reduce negative feelings or to address personal problems

The VFI is best used in a comparative way—to understand, for example, how one set of functions might be considered more important than another, or how the motivations of non-volunteers might differ from volunteers, or those of younger volunteers from older volunteers. In practical terms, the resulting "profiles" help organizations understand how to design volunteer programs that speak to the needs of their particular volunteers. Past independent tests of the VFI on various groups of volunteers find that these motivational categories can be useful in understanding differences between volunteers and non-volunteers, how volunteering histories might influence volunteer behavior, and how demographic patterns influence the motivation to volunteer (Allison, Okun, and Dutridge 2002; Esmond and Dunlop 2004; Greenslade and White 2005). These connections, in turn, offer the volunteer manager help in identifying the most effective volunteer resources for his or her association.

In this study, we use the VFI in several ways. We compare the reasons that respondents provide for their community-based volunteering (to churches, schools, etc.) to the reasons they provide for cosponsor association volunteering. We also compare volunteers to non-volunteers and

---

The Volunteer Functions Inventory

This was asked twice in the survey, first about community volunteering and then about association volunteering:

How important or accurate would the following statement be for you in doing volunteer work?

(rated on a five-point scale, with 1=Not at all important to 5=Very important)

a. I can do something for a profession or cause that is important to me
b. I can explore my own strengths
c. I can learn new skills through direct, hands-on experience
d. I can make new contacts that might help my business or career
e. I feel compassion toward people in need
f. I feel it is important to help others
g. Volunteer experience will look good on my resume
h. Volunteering allows me to gain a new perspective on things
i. Volunteering brings me satisfaction and recognition that I do not get at work
j. Volunteering can help me get my foot in the door at a place where I would like to work
k. Volunteering gives a competitive advantage to my business
l. Volunteering helps me deal with some of my own problems
m. Volunteering helps me to explore different career options
n. Volunteering is an important activity to the people I respect
o. Volunteering makes me feel needed

---

make some demographic comparisons. In past applications of the VFI, age groups emphasize different sets of motivations, gender differences influence volunteer motivations, and volunteers express stronger motivations than non-volunteers (Fletcher and Major 2004; Papadakis, Griffin, and Frater 2004). Researchers also find a connection between the activities volunteers engage in and their motivational profiles, indicating that motivations drive task preferences (Houle, Sagarin, and Kaplan 2005).

Strengths and Limitations of This Study

Before turning to our findings, we offer a final word about the strengths and limitations of this study. This study represents the largest and most comprehensive survey to date of association members and their volunteering behavior. It was designed and implemented using recommended practices, including stratified random sampling to include both known and unknown volunteers, an Internet-based questionnaire to improve survey completion rates, a validated mailing list of current cosponsor members, multiple requests to complete the survey, and rotated question ordering to reduce response bias. Many of the key survey questions had been tested and refined in prior studies. Except where we changed the wording of questions to capture cosponsor volunteering in particular (a largely unexplored area for volunteerism research), we maintained the original wording of all questions. The survey was pretested with association professionals. The participation of a large number of cosponsoring organizations, given the expected variation in their membership base, increases the generalizability of the data to the extent that our respondents are representative of members of similar organizations.

Although these procedures increase the reliability and validity of the results, all surveys are subject to some sampling error (caused by predictable variation between sampling frames) when they depend on a random selection of respondents rather than the full universe of possible subjects. However, even with a response rate of 14 percent, it is not difficult with a sampling frame of this magnitude to exceed expected confidence intervals of 95 percent. Our respondents reflect the characteristics of the full sampling frame with a margin of error of less than 1 percent.

Of greater concern with a study of this kind is the possibility of some non-sampling error (i.e., error built into the study design). Non-sampling errors of various kinds occur to some extent in all studies but can be minimized. Although our methods described above reduce the likelihood of major problems, we note here several potential causes of response bias in this survey. First, respondents will interpret questions differently, and some may also be unwilling to provide correct information (see especially a lower response rate on the personal demographic questions). Respondents may also be unable to recall information accurately about their volunteering history (see especially a low level of recall about how respondents were first recruited into volunteering). In addition, we used two approaches in this survey that may increase selection bias by dissuading some members from participating: the survey is rather lengthy, and it was timed for the holiday season. Even the use of each individual association's logo and mailing list to distribute the survey—although it can increase response rates because of higher credibility—can also increase the likelihood of selection bias because some members might be more prone than others to ignore association email. However, if the response bias that results is unpatterned, the harm is minimal.

Finally, as noted earlier, selection bias is built into surveys of volunteering behavior, since these surveys tend to elicit a greater response from the existing volunteers than the non-volunteers. We anticipated this result by designing a study that relies principally on within-sample comparisons (e.g., older members compared to younger members). Prior studies have also taught us how to avoid the worst impact of the "social desirability" factor: Since respondents could indicate that they volunteer more than they actually do, a recommended practice is to ask questions about the nature of volunteering in more than one way and to ask for the details of the volunteering activity.

Generally, these methodological limitations are minor, but they do suggest that you use caution in assuming that your own members would respond in a manner similar to those who participated in THE DECISION TO VOLUNTEER study. Given the scope of this study, we are confident that the results will be highly useful to the field of association management.

CHAPTER 3

The Big Picture

A S DESCRIBED IN CHAPTER 1, two principal objectives of our study were to identify association volunteers and to compare association volunteering to community volunteering. This chapter provides a summary profile of all survey respondents. It reports on volunteers' general characteristics and voluntary activity, draws comparisons where relevant to more general studies of U.S. volunteers, and examines motivations for volunteering, both in associations and in other community activities. Subsequent chapters (4 through 8) report on association volunteering in particular, focusing on how our survey respondents support the sponsoring organizations to which they belong. Chapter 9 discusses those individuals who do not volunteer, focusing on recruitment and retention strategies.

Demographic Characteristics

Of the more than 20,000 survey respondents who reported that they volunteered during the past 12 months (92.2 percent of all respondents), slightly more were male than female (Exhibit 3.1). The median age was 49 (Exhibit 3.2), principally representing the Gen X and Baby Boomer age groups. About four in five of our respondents are married or partnered (Exhibit 3.3) and have other family members who volunteer (Exhibit 3.4). More than half have no children living at home (Exhibit 3.5). The racial/cultural composition is not representative of the U.S. population in that minority groups are underrepresented (Exhibit 3.6). Most respondents (89.2 percent) answered from locations in the United States but 1 in 10 respondents were in worldwide locations outside the United States (Exhibit 3.7).

As you examine this profile of THE DECISION TO VOLUNTEER survey respondents, please keep in mind that this is an aggregate picture of a sampling frame that is quite diverse. As noted in Chapter 2, each of the 23 sponsoring organizations—and your organization—will have a unique membership profile whose characteristics should be taken into account as you draw your conclusions from this information.

EXHIBIT 3.1

Gender

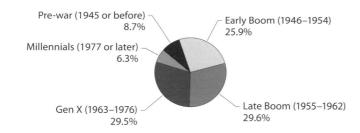

EXHIBIT 3.2

Age

EXHIBIT 3.3

Marital Status

EXHIBIT 3.4

Immediate Family Member Volunteers

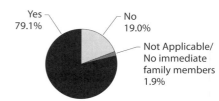

EXHIBIT 3.5

Children at Home

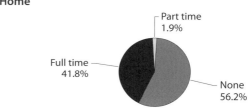

EXHIBIT 3.6

Race (U.S. respondents only)

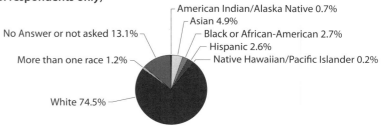

EXHIBIT 3.7

World Location

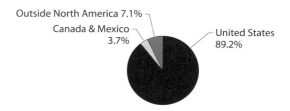

Occupation, Career Status, and Education

With respect to their occupations and education, the majority (88.9 percent) of our respondents are employed full time, while 6.6 percent are employed part time. An additional 1.6 percent are between jobs, and 2.8 percent are retired (Exhibit 3.8). About half are employed in the private sector, and one fifth are in the academic/educational fields; the remainder are in the nonprofit or government sectors, or are self-employed (Exhibit 3.9).[1] Most respondents are at mid-career level or senior level (Exhibit 3.10); this figure excludes those in education and those who are self-employed or unemployed).[2] More than half of our respondents have been in their profession since before 1990, with an average career length of 20 years (Exhibit 3.11).

A broad range of educational levels is represented among the survey respondents. One third hold a master's degree or equivalent, a further third hold a bachelor's degree, and the remainder are split nearly equally between those with less than a bachelor's degree and those with a doctoral degree or equivalent (Exhibit 3.12).

EXHIBIT 3.8

Employment Status

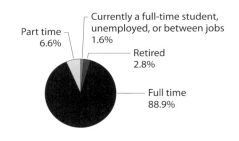

Part time
6.6%

Currently a full-time student, unemployed, or between jobs
1.6%

Retired
2.8%

Full time
88.9%

EXHIBIT 3.9

Sector (if employed full- or part time)

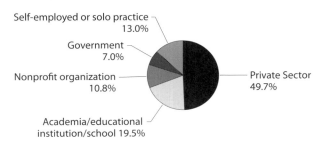

Self-employed or solo practice
13.0%

Government
7.0%

Nonprofit organization
10.8%

Private Sector
49.7%

Academia/educational institution/school 19.5%

EXHIBIT 3.10

Career Situation

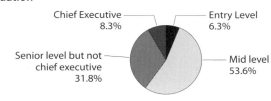

Chief Executive
8.3%

Entry Level
6.3%

Senior level but not chief executive
31.8%

Mid level
53.6%

EXHIBIT 3.11

Duration in Current Profession

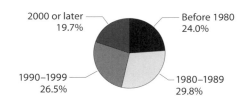

2000 or later
19.7%

Before 1980
24.0%

1990–1999
26.5%

1980–1989
29.8%

EXHIBIT 3.12

Education[3]

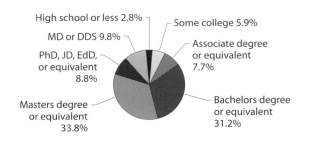

High school or less 2.8%

Some college 5.9%

MD or DDS 9.8%

Associate degree or equivalent
7.7%

PhD, JD, EdD, or equivalent
8.8%

Masters degree or equivalent
33.8%

Bachelors degree or equivalent
31.2%

---

[1] We recognize that these fields overlap, since a respondent can be in the nonprofit or public sectors and also in education.

[2] Note that throughout this book, we round to the nearest decimal. Not all figures total 100%.

[3] Note that for space considerations, we were not able to include all possible degree choices in the survey. Respondents were asked to choose the closest equivalent to their degree.

Volunteering Activity

Three quarters (77.1 percent) of respondents reported volunteering for any organization in the past 12 months, 15.1 percent reported volunteering in the past but longer than 12 months ago, and the remainder reported never volunteering. Exhibit 3.13 shows how this compares with volunteering for the cosponsor organization. In this section we mainly discuss the three quarters of respondents who are current volunteers for any organization.

EXHIBIT 3.13

Volunteering for Any Organization and Volunteering for Cosponsor Compared

In the last 12 Months — 77.1% Any organization / 36.4% Cosponsor organization

In the past but not in the last 12 Months — 15.1% Any organization / 8.7% Cosponsor organization

Never — 7.8% Any organization / 54.9% Cosponsor organization

Exhibit 3.14 compares in rank order the community activities for which members volunteer. Civic and community service is ranked first, followed by religious organizations, professional, and educational service. By comparison, the Bureau of Labor Statistics survey found that Americans over 25 years old volunteer for organizations in this order: religious (36.4 percent), educational or youth service (25.5 percent), social or community service (13 percent), hospital or health (7.8 percent), and civic/political/professional (5.3 percent).

The most common volunteer roles, in rank order, according to the BLS, are fundraising (11 percent), tutoring (10.8 percent), collecting or distributing food (9.5 percent), and professional assistance or board service (8.4 percent). In our survey of association professionals, the rank order was quite different: board service (57.2 percent), direct service such as food distribution or ushering (44.4 percent), coaching/tutoring (40.5 percent), organizing groups and meetings (40.2 percent), and fundraising (38.3 percent) (results not shown).

EXHIBIT 3.14

Which of the following best describes the type(s) of organizations for which you volunteered in the last 12 months?

Respondents checked all that apply. Shown in order with the most frequently reported type of organization first.

	%	Rank
Civic, community service	47.7	1
Religious	45.1	2
Professional, technical, or trade	42.1	3
Educational or youth service	41.0	4
Sport, hobby, cultural, or arts	26.4	5
Nonprofit health organization other than hospital or clinic	14.7	6
Hospital or clinic	8.7	7
Environmental or animal care	6.5	8
Political group or party	5.4	9
Public safety	4.2	10

Comparing our respondents to those in the BLS national survey of volunteering, the respondents to our survey provided a median of 50–99 hours of total volunteer service in the last twelve months (Exhibit 3.15). BLS survey respondents report a similar level, with a median of 54 annual hours. Our survey respondents (who include both U.S.-based members and members from other nations) are also comparable to those of the BLS in terms of the most active volunteers: 34.4 percent of our respondents report volunteering 100 or more hours in the past year, compared to 36.2 percent with the BLS.

Comparing the total hours our respondents volunteer against the hours they volunteer for their professional association, we find that most of their volunteer hours go to other organizations. The median hours donated to cosponsoring organizations are less than 12 per year. Four out of five respondents who volunteer for a cosponsor are contributing fewer than 50 hours per year. Just six percent are contributing 100 or more hours to their cosponsor, but five times that number give 100 or more hours to other organizations.

EXHIBIT 3.15

Approximately how many total hours did you perform volunteer work for [cosponsor] in the last 12 months?

| | Decision to Volunteer | | Bureau of Labor Statistics 2007* |
| | Volunteering for ANY organization | Volunteering for cosponsor | |
	%	%	%
1–12 hours	12.2	57.2	20.3
13–49 hours	28.3	26.5	23.6
50–99 hours	25.1	10.2	15.7
100–249 hours	22.1	4.4	
250–499 hours	7.7	1.2	30.1
500 or more hours	4.6	0.6	6.1

*The BLS Current Population Survey collects hours volunteered in these categories: 1–14 hours, 15–49, 50–99, 100–499, and 500 or more.

EXHIBIT 3.16

For how many different organizations did you perform volunteer work in the last 12 months?

| | Decision to Volunteer | Bureau of Labor Statistics 2007 |
	%	%
One	18.8	68.8
Two	31.3	19.7
Three	28.3	7.3
Four	12.4	2.5
Five or more	9.1	1.4

EXHIBIT 3.17

For how many different organizations did you perform volunteer work in the last 12 months?

| | Those who report volunteering but NOT for a cosponsor | Those who report volunteering for a cosponsor |
	%	%
One	12.6	23.0
Two	28.4	33.2
Three	31.7	26.1
Four	15.3	10.5
Five or more	12.0	7.2

Clearly, associations face a challenge in competing for the time and attention of those members who already volunteer elsewhere. The extent of the challenge becomes more apparent when we examine three more data comparisons. The table displayed as Exhibit 3.16 reflects the number of organizations for which respondents report volunteering compared with national studies. The Bureau of Labor Statistics reported from its 2007 study of volunteering that 68.8 percent of volunteers supported just one organization, 19.7 percent volunteered for two organizations, 7.3 percent volunteered for three, 2.5 percent volunteered for four, and 1.4 percent volunteered for five or more organizations in the past 12 months. In contrast, DECISION TO VOLUNTEER respondents appear to be much more heavily engaged in volunteering: About half volunteer for one or two organizations, and the other half of our sample volunteer for three or more organizations. More than 9 percent volunteer for five or more organizations, compared to the BLS average of 1.4 percent. This comparison signifies that our association members have a lot of organizations vying for their volunteer time.

A slightly different comparison, displayed in Exhibit 3.17, pits the organizational commitments of respondents who currently volunteer for the cosponsor against those who volunteer elsewhere. This comparison helps us to understand whether there is an opportunity for association professionals to tap volunteers who are involved in other community activities (ideally, under-involved so that they can be tapped for association activities). First the good news is that just 12.6 percent of respondents who volunteered in the past 12 months reported volunteering for only one organization. That level of volunteering could perhaps leave room for some additional activity. If approached with meaningful tasks and a sound recruitment strategy, these members could be potential new volunteers for an association. In fact, when asked if they volunteer to contribute to their workplace skills, nearly three quarters answered "yes." Excluding from this analysis those who currently volunteer for their association, this figure drops only slightly to 67 percent. This means that two thirds of those individuals who already volunteer, but not for the cosponsor, are still looking for opportunities to connect their volunteer work to their professional world, especially to build their skills. Such findings suggest there is untapped potential to increase your volunteer base by recruiting from among your members—although to succeed you will have to compete for the attention of busy people.

Who Is Volunteering for Associations?

As explained in Chapter 2, when we conducted this study, we combined (using a weighting factor) a random sample of members and a complete list of all known association volunteers. "Known" volunteers are those members who were identified in a cosponsor database as a volunteer. Below we compare the responses of those who were identified as known volunteers (identified by the cosponsor) to those who self-identified as volunteers by checking one or more of 20 activities described in the questionnaire.

We found that many more association members are volunteering for a cosponsoring organization than are known, and a few that are considered by the cosponsor to be volunteers do not report any current volunteer activity for the organization. Overall, a total of 36.4 percent of the survey respondents report volunteer activities for the cosponsor. Of these respondents, only 6.8 percent were identified by a cosponsor as a volunteer. The volunteers who were not identified by a cosponsor—the self-identified volunteers—perform a wide variety of services on behalf of the cosponsor, especially mentoring, professional advice, and membership recruitment (Exhibit 3.18). This finding is of some concern, since formal record-keeping of volunteer activity is considered to be an essential first step in building an effective volunteer program (Hager and Brudney 2004).

Two thirds of those individuals who already volunteer, but not for the cosponsor, are still looking for opportunities to connect their volunteer work to their professional world. Such findings suggest there is untapped potential to increase your volunteer base by recruiting from among your members.

EXHIBIT 3.18

In the last 12 months, have you done any of the following as a volunteer (in person, online, or in any other way) on behalf of [cosponsor]?
Respondent checked all applicable.

	Cosponsor Volunteers			
	Identified by cosponsor		Self-identified	
	%	Rank	%	Rank
Served on a committee for a local chapter or section	10.2	4	37.2	1
Recruited a member or members	11.7	3	35.1	2
Provided mentoring, coaching, or tutoring for members, students, or others	13.7	1	34.9	3
Spoke or presented a paper	8.1	6	34.2	4
Served on the board for a local chapter or section	6.6	7	31.8	5
Provided professional advice	12.8	2	31.6	6
Reviewed a paper or proposal for a publication	5.1	10	30.1	7
Served on a committee for the parent organization	3.9	14	29.6	8
Participated in a discussion group, expert panel, or report	8.2	5	28.1	9
Served on a technical committee or reviewed standards and practices	3.9	15	26.9	10
Moderated or facilitated discussion groups at meetings or elsewhere	5.8	8	26.1	11
Submitted a paper or manuscript for publication	4.4	11	25.7	12
Reviewed proposals for conferences or projects	4.0	12	23.9	13
Reviewed research, conducted literature review or resource reviews, or analyzed data	3.9	13	14.9	14
Raised funds	5.7	9	14.6	15
Wrote proposals, grant applications, or business plans	2.6	17	9.1	16
Reviewed applications as part of accreditation, certification, or competitive program	3.0	16	8.8	17
Served on the board for the parent organization	1.4	19	7.2	18
Made a presentation or testified on behalf of the organization to any legislative body (local, state, national, or global advocacy)	2.2	18	6.4	19
Prepared background for regulators, the press, or others	1.4	20	4.8	20

How Do Association Members Become Volunteers?

Many of the volunteers in our study did not recall the means by which they were recruited to cosponsor volunteering (Exhibit 3.19). However, for those who did, the most common means were being asked by another volunteer (13.3 percent of all responses), recruited at a meeting (13.4 percent of all responses), or invited through a local chapter (14.2 percent of all responses). It is noteworthy to observe here that few respondents contacted the organization themselves and offered to volunteer. It takes organizational effort to identify willing members and solicit their help. This advice is consistent with national studies of giving and volunteering, which also find that most volunteers and donors must first be asked to participate.

EXHIBIT 3.19

How did you first learn about the volunteer opportunities available to you through [cosponsor]? Please select only one.
Shown in order with most frequent response first.

	%
I don't recall	26.6
Through a local chapter or section	14.2
At a meeting, conference, or other event	13.4
I was asked by another volunteer	13.3
A staff member of the organization asked me to volunteer	8.9
I answered a call/ad for volunteers	5.1
Through my employer (current or past)	5.1
Through a professor or someone at my university or school	3.7
Through a posting on their web site	3.0
I contacted the organization and offered to volunteer	2.8
I saw an advertisement in the organization's magazine or other publication	2.3
Other way	1.6

Satisfaction with Association Volunteering

This section of the chapter reports on several questions we posed to those who volunteer for a cosponsor about their satisfaction with their cosponsor volunteer experiences. In subsequent chapters, we will compare members to one another to see whether age, experience, career level, amount of service, or other factors influence their responses.

In Exhibit 3.20, responses are given on a scale of 1 (very dissatisfied) to 5 (very satisfied). The mean is reported in the table, where responses above 3.00 indicate more satisfaction than dissatisfaction with the experience.

We find here a reflection of the self-serving and other-serving motivations behind volunteer work discussed in Chapter 2. Cosponsor volunteers are highly satisfied with their ability to provide other-serving benefits to their profession, such as giving back (ranked first), working toward a common goal (ranked third), and connecting to the mission of the organization

EXHIBIT 3.20

How satisfied are you with the following aspects of your volunteer experience with [cosponsor]?
Mean shows the average rating on a 1–5 scale with 5=very satisfied. Shown in order with highest satisfaction first.

	Mean	Rank
Helping you to feel that you are giving back to your profession	3.86	1
Having opportunities to meet, work, and socialize with others in your field or profession	3.83	2
Working with others toward a common goal	3.78	3
Using your existing skills	3.74	4
Feeling respected, appreciated, and valued	3.59	5
Opportunity to take a leadership role	3.58	6
Ability to make choices about when you volunteer	3.54	7
Helping you to connect with the mission of the organization	3.52	8
Ability to make choices about what you do as a volunteer	3.51	9
Learning new skills	3.45	10
Receiving feedback about your performance	3.20	11
Receiving training needed to be effective	3.18	12
Receiving incentives like stipends, transportation, and/or meals	2.82	13

(ranked eighth). But members also seek more tangible benefits through volunteerism. For professional volunteering, they are most satisfied with their ability to meet, work, and socialize with others in their profession (ranked second), use their skills (ranked fourth), and take a leadership role (ranked sixth). Finally, we see evidence of effective association practices when members report that they feel respected and appreciated and are given choices about when they volunteer or what they do. The areas that seem most ripe for improvement include incentives, training, and feedback for volunteers.

The following tables report on answers to questions about the impact volunteering has had on respondents' careers (Exhibit 3.21), their overall satisfaction with volunteering for the cosponsor (Exhibit 3.22), their interest in future cosponsor volunteering (Exhibit 3.23), and their likelihood of encouraging other members to cosponsor volunteering (Exhibit 3.24).

As shown in Exhibit 3.21, most respondents report that volunteering has had a very positive impact on their career, with three quarters reporting a positive to very positive impact of volunteering in general. When we turn to cosponsor volunteering in particular, we see that the satisfaction, interest in future volunteering, and willingness to recommend volunteering are moderately correlated with one another (at 50–70 percent). The most positive response comes with Exhibit 3.22, where more than half of respondents report that they are satisfied to very satisfied with their cosponsor

volunteering experience. About a third (36.4 percent) are ambivalent, and just 8.3 percent are unhappy with the experience. However, the trouble starts in the next two questions. Half of the respondents are unlikely to continue volunteering in another year, one quarter are likely, and one quarter are ambivalent (Exhibit 3.23). On whether they would recommend volunteering to a friend or colleague, the responses are more balanced, but more respondents still indicate that they would be unlikely to recommend cosponsor volunteering than those who would (Exhibit 3.24). These responses will be of some concern to associations, and we explore strategies for improving satisfaction with volunteering in subsequent chapters.

What Motivates Volunteers?

As we discussed in Chapter 2, researchers have developed some common measurement instruments for assessing the relative benefits that volunteers look for in their volunteer work (such as an opportunity to help others, to develop new skills, etc.). We employ in this survey an instrument called the Volunteer Functions Inventory that has been widely tested and has a good connection to the professional benefits of volunteering (Clary, Snyder et al. 1998). The rather unusual wording of some of these questions is because this instrument was developed as a psychological tool, based on the way people might express their desire to volunteer. Throughout this book, as we

EXHIBIT 3.21

What effect do you think volunteering has had on your career or, if you are self-employed, on your business?
Asked of all those who volunteer for an association or anywhere else. (Do not know excluded)

	%
Very negative	0.2
2	0.9
3	15.3
4	29.7
Very positive	54.0

EXHIBIT 3.22

Please use the scale provided below to rate your overall satisfaction with volunteering for [cosponsor].
Asked only of cosponsor volunteers. (No response excluded)

	%
Very dissatisfied	1.7
2	6.6
3	36.4
4	36.5
Very satisfied	18.9

EXHIBIT 3.23

How likely is it that you will be a volunteer for [cosponsor] within the next 12 months?
Asked of all respondents. (No response excluded)

	%
Very unlikely	27.9
2	21.3
3	25.3
4	12.1
Very likely	13.4

EXHIBIT 3.24

How likely is it that you would recommend volunteering for [cosponsor] to a friend or colleague?
Asked of all respondents. (No response excluded)

	%
Very unlikely	19.4
2	18.2
3	30.8
4	17.6
Very likely	13.9

compare members to one another on some key demographic differences, we will also be comparing their responses to the VFI.

To begin we compare in Exhibit 3.25 the aggregate responses of members who perform community volunteering to those who perform cosponsor volunteering. The two samples overlap with one another slightly. We asked this set of questions twice in the survey (and we thank the survey participants for their patience). We first asked them to assess the reasons they volunteer in terms of their community volunteering, and we then asked them to assess the same reasons in terms of cosponsor volunteering. The benefit of this approach is in helping us understand whether association volunteering has its own unique characteristics or drivers.

We expected to find that association members are more interested in the career-related reasons for volunteering when they are volunteering for their professions in comparison to their community volunteering. And we do find this connection, where respondents rank questions within the "Career" dimension higher for association volunteering than for community volunteering. But we also find that the relative ranking of each dimension to another does not change: Agreement with the questions related to the Values dimension—reflecting the desire to help others, support a cause or profession, and act on compassionate instincts—is weaker for association volunteering but still ranked most important for any kind of volunteering. The other important lesson from this comparison is that members do not generally feel as strongly about their reasons for association volunteering as they do for community volunteering. This result suggests that associations will have to work harder than charities to communicate the professional and societal value of association volunteering.

The survey information that will be most useful to associations as they consider the strength of their volunteer program is the following:

- Three quarters of our survey respondents currently volunteer in the community, but only one third volunteer for an association that sponsored this survey.

- Substantially more association members volunteer for cosponsors than are actually tracked by cosponsors.

- The majority of our cosponsors are in highly desirable demographic and socio-economic groups for increased volunteer activity, but they

EXHIBIT 3.25

Volunteer Functions Inventory (VFI)*

Regardless of your previous volunteer experience, how important or accurate would the following statements be for you in doing volunteer work?

		Total	
		Volunteering in general	Volunteering for cosponsor
VFI Dimensions		Mean	Mean
Values	I feel it is important to help others	4.38	3.89
	I can do something for a profession or cause that is important to me	4.12	3.94
	I feel compassion toward people in need	4.08	3.52
Understanding	Volunteering allows me to gain a new perspective on things	3.88	3.41
	I can explore my own strengths	3.41	3.24
	I can learn new skills through direct, hands-on experience	3.37	3.24
Enhancement	Volunteering makes me feel needed	3.17	2.73
	Volunteering brings me satisfaction or recognition that I do not get at work	3.12	2.67
Career	I can make new contacts that might help my business or career	2.70	2.89
	Volunteer experience looks good on my resume	2.37	2.50
	Volunteering helps me to explore different career options	2.23	2.37
	Volunteering gives a competitive advantage to my business	2.18	2.41
	Volunteering can help me get my foot in the door at a place where I would like to work	2.02	2.22
Social	Volunteering is important to the people I respect	3.30	3.09
Protective	Volunteering helps me deal with some of my own problems	2.29	2.08

* The VFI compares volunteers according to what they believe they gain through volunteer work. Mean shows the average rating on a 1–5 scale with 5=very important. The 15 questions were rated by respondents twice in the survey. First, all respondents were asked about "volunteering in general." Later in the survey, the same questions were asked of respondents who currently volunteer for the cosponsor OR who have volunteered for the cosponsor anytime in the past. Items are grouped according to the six underlying dimensions identified in the Volunteer Functions Inventory (see Bibliography: Clary, Snyder, and Stukas 1996).

are also more active volunteers generally than U.S. averages so have more demands on their time.

- Association members are looking for opportunities to connect their volunteer and professional work.

- Association members reflect the pro-social motivations of most volunteers in serving for generally altruistic reasons (supporting a cause), but also in expecting some personal benefits in return (growth, feedback, recognition).

- Although they are generally satisfied with their own volunteer experience, many members do not intend to continue volunteering for the cosponsor or to recommend volunteering to others.

ACTING ON THE FINDINGS
Preferences and Expectations

THE DECISION TO VOLUNTEER findings can be used to assess how your members are involved in association volunteer activities, with an overall assessment of the preferences and expectations of your particular members being an important first step. Findings discussed in this chapter might lead you to examine the following aspects of your volunteer management program:

- In addition to tracking the committee and governance services performed by volunteers, do you know and keep track of the various ad hoc or informal services they provide?

- Do you keep a history of volunteer involvement in your association so that you can detect a natural progression between formal, informal, or other levels of activity?

- When your volunteers "graduate" to higher levels of involvement, who moves forward and who drops out? Do you actively promote their involvement?

- How can this historical information help you build a volunteer recruitment and retention strategy?

- Can you identify members who might be looking for increased responsibilities?

- Can you identify volunteers who are close to burnout?

- Are you aware of your volunteer pool's contributions outside of your organization? For example, if you find your volunteers are tending to volunteer more frequently in community-based settings or organizations, in what way can you encourage volunteer opportunity through local components such as projects that benefit the community?

Considering Strengths
Understanding volunteers' strengths allows you to effectively match members to the volunteer opportunities you have available. Consider a self-evaluation tool that asks members to identify their strengths. Take time to reflect on how your association views—and values—ad hoc volunteering.

- Do you give ad hoc volunteering appropriate importance, visibility, and recognition?

- Do you recruit as actively for ad hoc volunteers as for committee and board positions?

Appealing to Values

The findings suggest that it may be more important to appeal to members' values than career benefits in motivating them to volunteer, but both may be important to some members.

- How can the "what's in it for me" message in your association be framed to attract a range of potential volunteers?
- How can the message be framed to address intangible benefits such as values?
- How do you communicate to your members the value of volunteering?
- Do you test your volunteer messages by asking potential volunteers what they see as the potential value?

Sharing Volunteers' Outcomes

Do you communicate to your membership and the industry at large how your volunteers have helped others and their profession? To strengthen the message, consider sharing a variety of specific examples of the outcomes your volunteers have experienced, both personally and professionally, to address the question "what's in it for me?"

- How do you welcome your new volunteers and how do you introduce your staff to them?
- Would your staff and board recognize a prominent volunteer if they met one?
- Are your staff trained and socialized to work effectively with volunteers?

Calculating the Value of Volunteers

Do you know the value of volunteer labor to your organization? Do you know how much it costs to replace a volunteer who leaves? Many associations struggle to quantify the return on investment of their volunteer program. Survey your volunteer pool to determine the number of hours your volunteers commit to your organization. Calculate the hard costs needed to replace those unpaid people resources with a paid workforce. This resource from the Points of Light Foundation offers one way to calculate the economic value of volunteers: **www.pointsoflight.org/resources/research/calculator.cfm**

Some of the volunteers' contributions will be intangible, but this exercise provides a generalized perspective on the value of your volunteers. You can then evaluate whether your association is investing the appropriate funds needed to recruit, train, and reward this segment of your workforce.

CHAPTER 4

Level of Affiliation

WHAT SERVICES ARE ASSOCIATION volunteers performing for your organization or for other organizations? What personal or professional characteristics distinguish their level of activity and the services they perform? And how might these characteristics influence your members' interest in becoming more involved in association activities? In this chapter, we call these differences "levels of affiliation" to reinforce the point that your members, as volunteers, support organizational activities in multiple ways. Some are looking for leadership opportunities, others to expand their professional network, and others to pass on their knowledge to younger members.

Differences in their activities and levels of affiliation as volunteers stem from differences in their objectives and consequently influence your members' satisfaction with the volunteer experience. For example, those volunteers most centrally involved in your association, such as board and committee members, might have a very different experience with volunteering than those who are just getting started in their profession. Those who are involved at the local, chapter level will engage with your organization in ways that differ from those who provide leadership at the national level. Volunteers choose the activities that they want to be involved in, so it stands to reason that different patterns of volunteer engagement will emerge. And when we stop treating all volunteers alike, it is easier to understand how best to recruit them, involve them, recognize their contributions, and keep them engaged in the organization.

Distinct Patterns of Involvement

We began by grouping the association volunteers into categories according to the kinds of services they perform for their associations. We used a technique called a two-step cluster analysis to accomplish this task. This method, commonly used in marketing and consumer research, identifies the natural groupings and underlying patterns in large datasets that might not otherwise be apparent.

Our analysis created four categories of volunteers who are active in any of the 23 cosponsoring associations (Exhibit 4.1):[1]

EXHIBIT 4.1

Cosponsor Volunteer Activity Categories

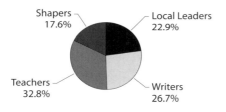

- **Local leaders** represent 22.9 percent of cosponsor volunteers. They focus their efforts on board and committee service at the local level and on mentoring and membership recruiting. They represent an important resource for association governance within component organizations, but they appear to be less centrally involved in governance in the parent organization. Nearly two thirds of this group come from the entry-level or mid-career levels of employment. This group is represented equally by employees across the private, nonprofit, and government sectors. In this group, 17.5 percent contribute 50 or more volunteer hours per year for the cosponsor, and 82.5 percent contribute 49 or fewer hours.

- **Writers** (26.7 percent) focus their energies on the review and publication of professional papers. They are likely to represent many of the subject matter experts in various fields, but they are much less involved in other association activities such as leadership, fundraising, or recruitment. They are slightly more likely to come from the government or private sectors, or to be self-employed. In this group, 88.4 percent contribute 49 or fewer volunteer hours per year to the cosponsor.

- **Teachers,** representing one third (32.8 percent) of all cosponsor volunteers, serve as important sources of professional advice, mentorship, and recruitment for their fellow members. Again, however, they are only minimally engaged in other areas. They are slightly more likely to work in the nonprofit rather than business sector, but their professional background is otherwise quite similar to the other groups. This group contributes the fewest volunteer hours for the cosponsor organization (95.1 percent contribute 49 or fewer hours per year).

- **Shapers** are the "super-volunteers," involved in virtually every area of association activity. The 17.6 percent of respondents who fell into this category perform the majority of volunteer work within the associations participating in this study. They are substantially more likely to come from academic backgrounds, and more than half of this group is employed at the senior executive level. They contribute the greatest number of volunteer hours to their association: 41.1 percent contribute 50 or more hours per year to the cosponsor.

The frequencies displayed in Exhibit 4.2 describe the percentage of individuals in each group who report that they perform an activity for their association. Activities that comprise the basis for each category are shown in bold.

We also looked at cosponsor volunteering as it is traditionally understood in associations: by level of responsibility. Volunteers serve associations at three general levels: as board members and elected leaders (governance), in ongoing responsibilities often organized around committee work (committee/ongoing), or on an as-needed basis (ad hoc). For comparison, these responsibilities are organized in Exhibit 4.3 according to the highest level of responsibility showing how they fall into our four new categories of involvement.

One of the chief distinctions among our four categories of volunteer involvement is in the kind of affiliation they have with the organization:

---

[1] Note in all cases that these individuals may contribute volunteer hours elsewhere.

EXHIBIT 4.2

In the last 12 months, have you done any of the following as a volunteer (in person, online, or in any other way) on behalf of [cosponsor]?

Respondents checked all applicable. Shown in percent of respondents who reported any volunteer activity with the cosponsor in the last 12 months.

	Local leaders		Writers		Teachers		Shapers	
	%	Rank	%	Rank	%	Rank	%	Rank
Provided professional advice	23.4	5	14.5	6	**43.6**	2	**74.8**	1
Provided mentoring, coaching, or tutoring for members, students, or others	**28.9**	4	11.9	8	**51.7**	1	**70.9**	2
Spoke or presented a paper	7.6	9	**38.7**	1	2.2	9	**64.7**	3
Participated in a discussion group, expert panel, or report	13.5	8	**24.7**	4	9.2	5	**64.5**	4
Moderated or facilitated discussion groups at meetings or elsewhere	14.3	7	10.3	10	4.7	7	**57.1**	5
Served on a committee for a local chapter or section	**83.0**	1	6.9	12	0.0	19	**52.2**	6
Recruited a member or members	**41.0**	3	6.9	13	**41.3**	3	**52.1**	7
Reviewed proposals for conferences or projects	3.6	13	10.0	11	1.5	13	**48.3**	8
Reviewed a paper or proposal for a publication	1.0	20	**26.4**	2	0.6	16	**47.4**	9
Reviewed research, conducted literature review or resource reviews, or analyzed data	1.3	17	11.5	9	2.7	8	**41.7**	10
Served on a committee for the parent organization	5.2	10	13.8	7	1.9	11	**40.6**	11
Served on the board for a local chapter or section	**55.2**	2	3.1	17	0.0	20	**36.9**	12
Submitted a paper or manuscript for publication	1.1	19	**26.1**	3	0.3	18	**36.8**	13
Served on a technical committee or reviewed standards and practices	3.4	14	19.0	5	1.3	14	**35.4**	14
Raised funds	22.8	6	2.7	18	13.1	4	**34.9**	15
Wrote proposals, grant applications, or business plans	1.4	16	5.6	14	2.1	10	**29.7**	16
Reviewed applications as part of accreditation, certification, or competitive program	5.1	11	3.3	16	5.2	6	**28.0**	17
Made a presentation or testified on behalf of the organization to any legislative body (local, state, national, or global advocacy)	4.6	12	4.7	15	1.1	15	21.4	18
Served on the board for the parent organization	1.3	18	2.5	19	0.6	17	17.7	19
Prepared background for regulators, the press, or others	1.8	15	1.3	20	1.9	12	16.1	20

* Activities in **bold** identify the high incidence activities in that cluster. Descriptions of ad hoc activities are shown in *italics*.

The Local Leaders and Shapers are the most *formally* involved in association activities through board and committee work; the Writers and Teachers are more likely to perform activities that are *ad hoc* in nature and less likely to serve the organization in governance and committee activities. Our point here is not to make any distinction among these responsibilities in terms of their value to an organization. For example, membership recruitment at your organization might or might not be supported or recognized formally, but even as an *ad hoc* activity, it has tremendous strategic importance. Our point is to observe that differences among these groups in levels of activity will be important to you from a volunteer management perspective, because those volunteers with formal roles in the organization may be easier to identify and support than those without. Volunteers who serve an organization through *ad hoc* activities alone require additional organizational effort to track, support, and recognize for their efforts. If these *ad hoc* volunteers are not recognized for their efforts, they may feel less appreciated.

EXHIBIT 4.3

Cosponsor Level of Volunteering by Cosponsor Volunteer Category

	Local leaders	Writers	Teachers	Shapers
	%	%	%	%
Governance[1]	55.6	5.5	0.7	45.5
Committee/Ongoing[2]	43.8	31.1	3.0	36.4
Ad Hoc[3]	0.7	63.4	96.3	18.1

[1] These are volunteers who serve on boards either at the local or the parent level.

[2] These are volunteers who serve on committees at the local or parent level.

[3] These are volunteers who serve in one or more of the ways shown in *italics* in Exhibit 4.2 but do NOT also serve on the Board or committee level.

Demographic Patterns

The demographic characteristics of the cosponsor volunteers within the four groups are compared below along with the demographics of those who have not volunteered for the cosponsor in the last 12 months (63.6 percent of all respondents). Exhibit 4.4 displays gender differences across volunteer groups. We observe an even dispersion between men and women among

Local Leaders and Teachers, whereas men predominate in the Writers and Shapers groups and among those not currently volunteering for the cosponsor. In national volunteering studies, women volunteer substantially more than men regardless of employment status, marital status, or number of children.[2] In national studies, however, men volunteer more hours in certain activities such as board service (BLS 2008). In our analysis of cosponsor volunteers, we see a somewhat similar pattern in that Writers and Shapers (who are heavily involved in governance) are more likely to be male than are Local Leaders and Teachers. We find very little difference among these categories in other demographic comparisons, including race, employment status, marital, or family status of the respondents (results not shown).

EXHIBIT 4.4

Gender by Cosponsor Volunteer Category

	Local leaders	Writers	Teachers	Shapers	Not a current cosponsor volunteer
	%	%	%	%	%
Male	46.7	64.7	49.5	61.4	57.5
Female	53.3	35.3	50.5	38.6	42.5

Exhibits 4.5 and 4.6 organize volunteers and non-volunteers according to age group and educational level. Ages are grouped into five major generations according to birth date. Not at all surprisingly, the Shapers, representing many of the leaders and the most heavily engaged volunteers, are slightly older in average age than other volunteer groups. Overall, non-volunteers are generally younger than volunteers. Nonetheless, a substantial proportion of the youngest two generations (Gen X and Millennials) are well represented in the four active cosponsor groups: Volunteers younger than 45 represent nearly one quarter (24.9 percent) of the Shapers and 30–34 percent of the Local Leaders, Writers, and Teachers. If you are eager to tap these younger generations, you will find substantial opportunities to do so.

---

[2] In the 2007 Survey of Volunteering by the Bureau of Labor Statistics, 42% of U.S. volunteers ages 25 or older were men, and 58% were women.

As for educational level, volunteers in the Writers and Shapers groups are more likely to hold professional or advanced degrees (Exhibit 4.6).

EXHIBIT 4.5

Age by Cosponsor Volunteer Category

	Local leaders	Writers	Teachers	Shapers	Not a current cosponsor volunteer
	%	%	%	%	%
Pre-war (1945 or before)	8.3	11.2	11.3	14.9	7.3
Early Boom (1946–1954)	30.2	26.3	29.7	33.8	23.8
Late Boom (1955–1962)	28.2	28.6	29.9	27.4	30.0
Gen X (1963–1976)	26.6	29.9	24.2	22.0	31.6
Millennials (1977 or later)	6.7	4.0	4.9	1.9	7.3

EXHIBIT 4.6

Level of Education by Cosponsor Volunteer Category

	Local leaders	Writers	Teachers	Shapers	Not a current cosponsor volunteer
	%	%	%	%	%
Less than Bachelor's	22.4	10.1	19.4	12.6	16.5
Bachelor's Degree	28.2	21.9	28.2	17.8	34.8
Master's or PhD	40.1	53.5	42.9	53.5	40.1
Medical Doctor	9.3	14.5	9.5	16.1	8.5

Volunteer Recruitment

Across our four patterns of volunteer activity, we find some differences in the ways in which members learned about volunteering for their organizations (Exhibit 4.7). Among the chief differences, Local Leaders, Teachers, and Shapers were most likely to have been asked by another volunteer, while Writers more often answered a general call for volunteers. Teachers and Writers (who are involved in very little committee work) were less likely than Local Leaders and Shapers to have been asked to volunteer by

association staff. Finally, it stands to reason that Local Leaders, who are more involved at the chapter level, were considerably more likely to have been recruited at the chapter level as well.

EXHIBIT 4.7

How did you first learn about the volunteer opportunities available to you through [cosponsor}?
Only one answer was permitted.

	Local leaders	Writers	Teachers	Shapers	Not a current cosponsor volunteer
	%	%	%	%	%
Through a local chapter or section	25.0	6.9	8.8	12.0	20.1
I don't recall	16.5	30.6	45.3	25.3	17.8
I was asked by another volunteer	16.4	15.7	6.5	15.4	15.1
At a meeting, conference, or other event	14.3	13.6	11.4	13.8	14.2
A staff member of the organization asked me to volunteer	11.0	9.4	5.4	11.2	9.5
Through my employer (current or past) or professor	7.6	8.6	8.9	9.2	9.4
Through a call for volunteers, web site posting, or advertisement from the organization	6.5	12.3	12.2	9.7	7.2
I contacted the organization and offered to volunteer	2.9	3.0	1.5	3.5	3.6

Among the similarities, recruiting volunteers through meetings and conferences was an important method for volunteers at all four levels of activity. Also notable is how many volunteers across the four categories did not recall how they were recruited into volunteering. This fact limits our ability to understand what kinds of volunteer recruitment methods an association might be overlooking. Perhaps even more importantly, volunteers who lose track of the people or activities who first got them engaged in association volunteering might be missing a connection to an important resource and source of support. Keeping that connection could be helpful in keeping volunteers engaged.

Finally, volunteers are recruited into association activity through a variety of means. No single method accounts for more than 25 percent of total recruitment activity, although some means are more frequently reported in certain categories. The lesson from this finding is that your association should consider multiple ways of engaging members in volunteer activities. The same lesson, in fact, holds true for fundraising in the nonprofit sector. Donors make gifts in response to many different kinds of appeals, and many donors make multiple gifts in response to multiple appeals. You may find that communicating volunteer opportunities at your association in multiple ways, through multiple levels of the organization, succeeds in unanticipated ways. It can not only encourage new members to donate their time, but it can also help volunteers find the work that is right for them. But it is also important to note that volunteers (like donors) have to be asked: As observed in Chapter 3, few of these volunteers across the four groups offered to volunteer on their own initiative. It is the association's responsibility to take the initiative by making volunteer opportunities visible and attractive and by forwarding volunteer needs to the members at the front lines who can help with recruitment.

Why Members Volunteer

Exhibit 4.8 compares cosponsor volunteers according to what they believe they gain through volunteer work. Respondents were asked how important each of the following reasons was for performing volunteer work for the cosponsor, using a five-point scale. Their choices ranged from 1 for "not at all important" to 5 for "extremely important." The mean (average) responses are displayed, where the higher the mean response, the more strongly respondents felt that this particular reason for volunteering had value for them. The 15 questions asked of all respondents are displayed in rows, grouped according to the six underlying dimensions identified in the Volunteer Functions Inventory (Clary, Snyder, and Stukas 1996). The mean responses are displayed in columns, grouped according to the four categories of cosponsor activity plus an additional column for "Former cosponsor volunteers." This last category includes those who volunteered

for the cosponsor in the past but no longer volunteer for the cosponsor (some of whom volunteer elsewhere and some of whom do not presently volunteer).

The results demonstrate several interesting facts about why individuals are involved in association volunteering. First, individuals volunteer for many different reasons, an observation that applies to this study and many others. It is important to recognize that volunteers expect multiple, diverse benefits from their labor. Second, the Local Leaders and Shapers, as those who are more involved and invested in association success (based on hours donated), are also most likely to agree with the importance of volunteering. This difference is reflected in higher mean scores across all dimensions and questions for these two groups. We also note that the Career dimension is more important to Local Leaders than to others. This group represents slightly younger and highly motivated association volunteers who assign higher value to the professional benefits of volunteering.

Third, compared to current cosponsor volunteers, former cosponsor volunteers are less likely to find value in volunteering for cosponsor activities. The reason for this difference could rest on the presence of more individuals in the volunteer group who have had volunteer experiences generally and so recognize the value of volunteering, or it could rest on some distinction volunteers make between their cosponsor activity and community volunteering. In other words, we caution the reader not to infer that *all* former volunteers are less motivated to volunteer than current volunteers. Some may be highly motivated to volunteer for activities other than association activity.

Finally, the Values dimension—embodied in questions about supporting people and causes that are important to the volunteer—seems to be most important to all respondents when compared to the five other dimensions. Other researchers have made similar conclusions about the importance of this particular dimension across volunteer groups (Allison, Okun, and Dutridge 2002; Clary, Snyder, and Stukas 1996).[3] In our study of professional volunteers, respondents rank the Understanding and Social

---

[3] In other studies, however, the value placed on each dimension is sensitive to volunteer demographics, particularly age and gender. We explore some of these demographic distinctions in Chapter 6.

EXHIBIT 4.8

Volunteer Functions Inventory (VFI)*

Regardless of your previous volunteer experience, how important or accurate would the following statements be for you in doing volunteer work?

By Level of Affiliation

		TOTAL	Local leaders	Writers	Teachers	Shapers	Former cosponsor volunteers
		Mean	Mean	Mean	Mean	Mean	Mean
Values	I feel it is important to help others	3.89	4.00	3.76	3.95	4.11	3.69
	I can do something for a profession or cause that is important to me	3.94	4.06	3.92	3.85	4.25	3.73
	I feel compassion toward people in need	3.52	3.58	3.31	3.68	3.73	3.29
Understanding	Volunteering allows me to gain a new perspective on things	3.41	3.52	3.38	3.39	3.68	3.15
	I can explore my own strengths	3.24	3.39	3.19	3.29	3.46	2.89
	I can learn new skills through direct, hands-on experience	3.24	3.38	3.20	3.26	3.48	2.93
Enhancement	Volunteering makes me feel needed	2.73	2.83	2.63	2.79	2.93	2.50
	Volunteering brings me satisfaction or recognition that I do not get at work	2.67	2.75	2.64	2.66	2.92	2.44
Career	I can make new contacts that might help my business or career	2.89	3.11	2.94	2.81	2.98	2.63
	Volunteer experience looks good on my resume	2.50	2.65	2.55	2.49	2.61	2.20
	Volunteering helps me to explore different career options	2.37	2.50	2.35	2.46	2.43	2.08
	Volunteering gives a competitive advantage to my business	2.41	2.58	2.46	2.39	2.62	2.03
	Volunteering can help me get my foot in the door at a place where I would like to work	2.22	2.35	2.22	2.28	2.28	1.96
Social	Volunteering is important to the people I respect	3.09	3.23	3.04	3.08	3.40	2.75
Protective	Volunteering helps me deal with some of my own problems	2.08	2.16	2.05	2.16	2.22	1.82

*The VFI compares volunteers according to what they believe they gain through volunteer work. Mean shows the average rating on a 1–5 scale with 5=very important. The 15 questions were rated by respondents twice in the survey. First, all respondents were asked about "volunteering in general." Later in the survey, the same questions were asked of respondents who currently volunteer for the cosponsor OR who have volunteered for the cosponsor anytime in the past. Items are grouped according to the six underlying dimensions identified in the Volunteer Functions Inventory (see Bibliography: Clary, Snyder, and Stukas 1996).

dimensions next following the Values dimension. The order in which respondents rank these questions is noteworthy since the Career dimension might be considered to be more important in a sample of professional volunteers. However, overall, our respondents are less interested in the professional benefits of volunteering to themselves or their businesses than they are in their ability to support their profession or other people, or gain new skills and perspectives through volunteering. Thus, we find the motivations of these cosponsor volunteers to be similar to those of other volunteers outside of associations.

To summarize:

- Individuals volunteer for a variety of reasons, and for a combination of self-serving ("learning new skills") and other-serving ("helping a cause") purposes.

- Even in professional organizations, the more competitive, career-oriented reasons for volunteering may be less important to individuals than the desire to enhance skills and do something for a cause that is important to them.

- Those who are heavily involved in volunteering are most likely to agree with the importance of volunteering.

Satisfaction With Volunteering

The results displayed earlier in Exhibit 4.2 suggested that association volunteers have a strong preference for certain volunteer activities over others. As an association professional, you need to understand these preferences if you are to engage and retain these volunteers successfully. But these patterns can be deceiving if used to gauge a member's overall satisfaction with volunteering. It is possible that the volunteers upon whom these organizations rely for certain skills can become focused on these activities at the expense of other opportunities. And if they are relied on too heavily by their peers (a situation likely to occur particularly with the Shapers), these volunteers could more quickly approach the point of burnout. Our next level of analysis, employing several survey questions about volunteer satisfaction, examines the possibility of such a result.

Comparing Cosponsor Volunteers to Other Volunteers

When asked what effect volunteering has had on their career, volunteers across the board generally report a strong positive effect and little negative impact. Cosponsor volunteers are more likely to relate the experience positively to their career than those respondents who volunteer for other causes, and we find little difference among our four categories of cosponsor volunteers. Association volunteering is more likely to occur during work hours than community volunteering; it requires time and energy, and it may result in opportunity costs for members. This survey suggests that volunteering imposes few demands that members consider to be professionally harmful, and it offers many benefits that they consider supportive of their careers.

Comparing Current and Past Cosponsor Volunteers

Exhibit 4.9 compares individuals who are currently volunteering for a cosponsoring organization to those who have volunteered in the past but no longer volunteer for the cosponsor (they may be volunteering elsewhere). Those who have never volunteered for the cosponsor are excluded from this exhibit.

EXHIBIT 4.9

Please use the scale provided below to rate your overall satisfaction with volunteering for [cosponsor].
Asked only of cosponsor volunteers.

	Local leaders	Writers	Teachers	Shapers	Former cosponsor volunteers
	%	%	%	%	%
Very dissatisfied	1.0	1.7	1.2	.9	3.8
2	3.7	6.0	6.6	3.4	12.9
3	28.4	34.0	48.6	23.5	42.0
4	42.4	40.7	30.0	41.8	29.1
Very satisfied	24.4	17.6	13.7	30.3	12.2

Association volunteers are a pretty satisfied group, and current volunteers are happiest. Respondents who currently volunteer for a cosponsoring association express about half the level of dissatisfaction with volunteering that past cosponsor volunteers do. Current cosponsor volunteers were also more likely to express satisfaction with their volunteer experience than those who had volunteered for the cosponsor in the past.

Although generally quite satisfied, cosponsor volunteers are not uniformly so. Shapers (i.e., those who are most actively involved) were the most satisfied group: Nearly three quarters (72.1 percent) express satisfaction with volunteering by rating their satisfaction with the experience either 4 or 5 on the scale. Local Leaders are also quite satisfied (66.8 percent), followed by Writers (58.3 percent). Teachers are a more ambivalent group: While only 7.8 percent report they are dissatisfied (rating 1 or 2 on the scale), nearly half (48.6 percent) are neutral, and fewer than half (43.7 percent) are satisfied (ratings of 4 or 5). Association professionals should investigate the reasons for this difference themselves, but we suggest that one factor might be this group's lower level of involvement.

One area where we might expect to find a difference but do not is in the comparison of people who volunteer but not for the cosponsor to lapsed volunteers (people who do not currently volunteer but have in the past). Lapsed volunteers might be less likely to describe value in volunteer activities. We find, instead, little substantive difference between the responses of those who volunteer outside of association activities and those who have ceased volunteering for the cosponsor. Since there are no *never*-volunteers in this group (that is, people who have not volunteered either for the cosponsor or elsewhere), responses are shaped by past volunteer experiences. Even if they are not currently volunteering, respondents' past experiences seem to have been fairly positive.

If you are looking for new sources of volunteer support, take note of this fact, since lapsed volunteers may be willing to become active again under the right circumstances. Indeed, an old piece of conventional wisdom in volunteer management is to avoid writing off a lapsed volunteer since new volunteer opportunities regularly arise.

Comparing the Likelihood of Volunteering for the Cosponsor in the Near Future

Exhibit 4.10 compares current cosponsor volunteers and those who have not volunteered for the cosponsor in the last year on the question of future volunteer intentions. All respondents, regardless of the current or past cosponsor volunteer status, were asked how likely they were to volunteer for a cosponsor within the next 12 months.

EXHIBIT 4.10

How likely is it that you will be a volunteer for [cosponsor] within the next 12 months?
Asked of all respondents.

	Local leaders	Writers	Teachers	Shapers	Not a current cosponsor volunteer*
	%	%	%	%	%
Very unlikely	5.0	6.1	11.9	4.6	40.2
2	9.0	11.9	16.4	6.6	27.3
3	18.9	24.5	33.5	15.9	25.0
4	24.1	26.2	22.2	21.1	5.1
Very likely	42.9	31.3	16.0	51.8	2.4

* Includes both those who have volunteered for the cosponsor in the past (former cosponsor volunteers) and those who have never volunteered for the cosponsor.

Generally, current cosponsor volunteers are most likely to volunteer again. Nearly three quarters of Shapers (72.9 percent) and two thirds (67 percent) of Local Leaders indicate that they will volunteer for the cosponsoring organization in the next 12 months. However, only 57.5 percent of Writers and 38.2 percent of Teachers indicate they will do the same. Among those who have not volunteered for the cosponsor in the past 12 months, only 7 percent indicate that they are likely to volunteer for the cosponsor in the near future.

Is this good news or bad news? You can interpret these results in several ways. First, it is encouraging to find that the most heavily involved volunteers appear to be most willing and most likely to be called on again. Even so, while most respondents indicate an intention to continue volunteering, a good portion of the remainder is ambivalent or seems unlikely to volunteer in the future. And you may find some cause for alarm in expected turnover within the ranks of the most active volunteers ranging upwards from 10 percent to as much as 28 percent—although this figure is lower than the annual volunteer turnover rate of 33 percent reported by the Bureau of Labor Statistics (CNCS 2007).

We suggest further investigation before acting on these results since the reasons for not participating in volunteer activity can vary substantially. Keep in mind that our question about future volunteering is merely a question about intent; it should not be misconstrued as a question about willingness to volunteer. In other words, those who do not currently volunteer simply may not have been asked. Secondly, ending a voluntary activity can be *involuntary*—that is, some individuals may be facing term limits on a board seat or other reasons beyond their control for ending an activity.

Organizations wishing to follow up on this study can regularly poll their own active members to understand why they might stop volunteering. Overuse could be a factor (leading to burnout), but so could underuse (members do not intend to volunteer simply because they do not anticipate being called on). Retirement is another possibility, although perhaps a small one. We ran the same analysis after removing respondents who were born before 1946 (assuming for the moment that many of them expect to retire soon from their association volunteering) and found an increase in future volunteer plans of only two percent across the younger volunteer categories. And a decision not to renew membership in an association is also likely to terminate volunteer activity: In THE DECISION TO JOIN study (ASAE & The Center for Association Leadership 2007), 6 percent of respondents were unsure they would renew their membership in the next cycle.

Further, differences in satisfaction levels—particularly among the four categories of cosponsor volunteers—can be reflective of differences in how the individuals in each group are supported and recognized for their efforts. And if organizations' volunteer management practices vary substantially, both internally and in comparison to their peers, these differences in volunteer treatment are likely to be reflected in volunteer satisfaction with the organization.

Satisfaction With Specific Aspects of the Cosponsor Volunteer Experience

We also polled current and former cosponsor volunteers about their satisfaction with particular aspects of their cosponsor volunteer experience (Exhibit 4.11). Our objective here was to help association professionals understand which specific volunteer management tools might be most useful in supporting volunteers and which benefits to emphasize with new volunteers. Respondents were asked to indicate their level of satisfaction on a five-point scale, with 1 indicating "very dissatisfied" and 5 indicating "very satisfied." Scores above 3.00 indicate that the majority of respondents were satisfied with that aspect of their volunteer experience; scores below 3.00 indicate a higher level of dissatisfaction than satisfaction.

The results demonstrate, again, that the most satisfied volunteers are also those most involved in association activities. Former volunteers are less satisfied than current cosponsor volunteers, and Shapers are the most satisfied group overall. In other respects, there is little variance across the questions. Most respondents were slightly more satisfied than dissatisfied (scores in the 3.00 to 4.00 range) with their volunteer experience. They were most satisfied with the ability through volunteering to feel they were giving back to their profession, to meet, work, and socialize with others in their field or profession, to work with others toward a common goal, and to use their skills. On only one question were the majority of respondents slightly more dissatisfied than satisfied: receiving incentives like stipends, transportation, and/or meals. This response suggests that volunteers would appreciate receiving some minimal material forms of support for their labor.

Differences Among Volunteers

Not all volunteers are alike. They bring different preferences and expectations regarding the work they do and how they will be recognized for it. Our categorization of association volunteers into four clusters or "typical" groups highlights the differences in their work preferences and also points out the close association between the intensity of their investment in association activities and their overall satisfaction with volunteering. In

EXHIBIT 4.11

How satisfied are you with the following aspects of your volunteer experience with [cosponsor]?

Asked only of those who either reported performing one or more of the listed cosponsor volunteer activities listed in the last 12 months OR who reported volunteering for the copsonsor at some time in the past.

Mean shows the average rating on a 1–5 scale with 5=very satisfied.

	Local leaders		Writers		Teachers		Shapers		Former cosponsor volunteers	
	Mean	Rank	Mean	Rank	Mean	Rank	Mean	Rank	Mean	Rank
Having opportunities to meet, work, and socialize with others in your field or profession	4.06	1	3.77	2	3.64	4	4.12	2	3.64	1
Helping you to feel that you are giving back to your profession	4.01	2	3.84	1	3.75	1	4.13	1	3.60	2
Working with others toward a common goal	3.95	3	3.72	4	3.67	3	4.07	3	3.56	3
Using your existing skills	3.82	4	3.75	3	3.67	2	3.99	4	3.50	4
Opportunity to take a leadership role	3.81	5	3.44	9	3.42	9	3.92	5	3.37	5
Feeling respected, appreciated, and valued	3.76	6	3.55	5	3.52	6	3.81	6	3.33	6
Helping you to connect with the mission of the organization	3.67	9	3.48	7	3.41	10	3.79	7	3.29	7
Ability to make choices about when you volunteer	3.70	7	3.48	6	3.53	5	3.72	8	3.27	8
Ability to make choices about what you do as a volunteer	3.70	8	3.47	8	3.46	7	3.70	9	3.23	9
Learning new skills	3.57	10	3.42	10	3.43	8	3.67	10	3.17	10
Receiving feedback about your performance	3.31	11	3.15	11	3.22	11	3.40	11	2.93	11
Receiving training needed to be effective	3.29	12	3.12	12	3.22	12	3.38	12	2.89	12
Receiving incentives like stipends, transportation, and/or meals	2.89	13	2.79	13	2.79	13	2.95	13	2.70	13

a nutshell, the most active association volunteers also appear to be the happiest with the results. This is generally good news for associations.

The question then becomes how to involve the under-invested volunteers more successfully. We derive several important lessons from this analysis:

- Those who do not currently volunteer simply may not have been asked.
- Volunteers who serve an organization through largely informal, ad hoc activities may require additional organizational effort to track, support, and receive recognition for their efforts.

- Volunteers respond to a wide variety of motivations and incentives, but stipends or expense reimbursement might be more actively employed to keep some volunteers involved.

One final caveat: Our grouping of volunteers into four categories is useful in illustrating the differences in how volunteers support associations, but you should not assume that all volunteers will follow this mold. Volunteer management activities within your organization should always begin with an assessment of the preferences and expectations of your particular members.

Levels of Involvement

As this chapter of THE DECISION TO VOLUNTEER makes clear, people will engage in volunteer activities at different levels. All levels are important, so it is critical to determine whether your volunteer systems reflect that notion. Consider how the four categories of involvement (Local leaders, Shapers, Writers, and Teachers) apply in your organization. Are there other patterns that you need to take into account? When you compare your volunteers' level of activity within each category, how do your volunteer characteristics or activities resemble or differ from those in this survey?

Charting Involvement

A great way to begin analyzing levels of involvement is to conduct an assessment of your volunteers' level of activity. To gather this information, if not readily available, survey a sampling of volunteers on average hours spent volunteering for your organization.

Set up a chart as follows, with key attributes that reflect your volunteer pool. Add to or subtract from the involvement levels seen in THE DECISION TO VOLUNTEER (horizontal axis) as appropriate.

	Local leaders	Teachers	Writers	Shapers
Key activities they perform				
Average number of hours devoted				
Age				
Gender				
Level of education				
Employment environment				

Using this information, evaluate your overall program. Do you offer different levels of volunteer engagement opportunities (i.e., according to time commitment, expertise required, location, etc.)? Do you offer sufficient opportunities in each category? How diverse is your volunteer pool by age, gender, level of education, employment environment, and any other demographic or other characteristics that are important to your organization?

Given the preference by several subcategories of volunteers for ad hoc opportunities, evaluate your program for this type of work. As you do, consider which ad hoc positions draw the greatest interest and compare them to other volunteer positions to determine the most preferred attributes (e.g., length of time required, skill set required, type of task, organizational versus individual focus).

Then, take a look at key responsibility areas in which your organization needs help but in which you are under-resourced. Are there activities or responsibilities from larger roles such as governance and committee/ongoing segments that could be recreated as ad hoc activities? These could then be promoted to your members with a focused message designed to appeal to those typically more interested in short-term volunteering opportunities. As a further step, consider the following questions by volunteer "category."

Board and Governance Volunteers

- What is the average age, education level, job role, and career stage of your association's board of directors? Committee leaders? What activities are they involved in aside from governance? How are they the same or different from other volunteers?

- What motivates your association's board and committee members to volunteer? How similar and different are they to other volunteers in terms of the benefits they expect from association volunteering?

- What are the entry points for board and committee member involvement in your association? Are these entry points planned and managed?

- Ask your association's board and committee members what they find most/least satisfying about their involvement.

- Do your association's board and committee members feel overextended in their volunteer responsibilities? To what extent? What can you do to protect leaders against volunteer burnout?

- How can your association leverage the knowledge gained from the questions above to better target and manage volunteer leaders at the board and committee level?

Teachers and Writers

- Teachers and writers contribute the least amount of time but account for the largest percentage of volunteers. They are also more difficult to track. Do you know who your Teachers and Writers are?

- Why do they fall into this category? Time commitment? Task? Expertise or lack thereof? Other professional or family obligations? Can they be encouraged to take on a larger commitment?

- Are Teachers asked to serve on committees? Many don't report this but may be a good fit, as they are actively engaged in professional advising and mentoring.

- Writers do not report being actively involved in organizational functions such as preparing background material for regulators or the press or getting involved at the local level and so forth, yet, they represent a key group of subject matter experts. How can you get them more involved in a broader role?

- Since Teachers are involved in mentoring other members and professionals in your field, are their efforts focused where needed in your organization (such as the local level, where sections and chapters are often suffering from lack of qualified or experienced leaders)?

- Are you missing opportunities to engage Teachers and Writers in broader or more formal roles? Are you building into your volunteer program the steps to capture those who want a greater role?

Local Leaders and Shapers

- These two categories represent the most active volunteers and those with the highest level of satisfaction. In what ways can you involve them in telling your volunteer story and recruiting new members?

- Are the possible linkages between groups planned and directed in your organization—for example, to take advantage of the skill and dedication of Shapers to build association leadership at the local level?

- Do you have a monitoring process in place to help avoid burnout for these and all volunteers?

- Since Local Leaders and Shapers are heavily involved and serve in a diverse set of roles, they could be good trainers. If so, can you tap them—through training—to move from doer to delegator?

- Do you have a formal pathway from local to national volunteerism?

- Shapers are more likely to serve on national boards. Can you use the profile of the Shaper to find those members who are underrepresented on the board (e.g., gender, race) with the same profile? Could this help you create a more diverse governing body?

CHAPTER 5

Generations and Career Level

R ESEARCHERS AND POLICYMAKERS ALIKE are interested in age-related differences in how people volunteer. Not only do they seek to understand how generational differences might influence volunteering preferences (because differences require adjustments in volunteer recruitment and support strategies) but they also hope to predict future levels of voluntary activity. Some have expressed a concern (also noted in Chapter 2) that older individuals, who volunteer at greater rates and levels of activity than do younger age groups, might leave an irreplaceable void behind when they retire from volunteering. Observers, most notably Robert Putnam (2000), speculate that if civil society is not to be permanently damaged, we need a concerted national effort to encourage younger age groups to increase their own voluntary activity to fill this gap in personnel. Further, organizations will need to reinvent themselves, to develop new strategies to engage these younger cohorts in ways that are meaningful to them.

Other voices offer a more reassuring perspective. They suggest that volunteer activity varies across the course of an individual's life because it is largely a reflection of changing social, professional, and family situations. For example, younger volunteers may prefer youth-related activities such as tutoring, while older individuals choose activities linked to their professional and family roles such as coaching, mentoring, and board service. In other words, the differences in volunteer rates that we see across generations are more about volunteer preferences than about an overall disposition to volunteer or not. Once associations work out how to connect their needs with the preferences and characteristics of their member volunteers, they will also learn how to tap enough volunteer support to meet their organizational objectives.

Volunteer motivations will also vary by age and career level. The younger or less experienced volunteer may have a stronger desire for self-improvement, new experiences, and skill development, while the older volunteer may express more interest in service, social opportunities, and the chance to "give back." Organizations must understand the differences if they are to frame the right recruitment messages. Omoto, Snyder, and Martino (2000, page 195) call this "matching the message to the motivation of the recipient," and our use of the Volunteer Functions Inventory is tailor-made to explore some of these possible differences.

Finally, the capacity to volunteer will vary according to life course: The new parent may display an equally strong interest in community service when compared to the new retiree, but these two individuals will vary substantially in terms of the responsibilities they can assume. Organizations wishing to capture the time and talent of either kind of volunteer must be adept at offering enough flexibility of choice and organizational support to meet their quite different expectations. For example, the promising volunteer who prefers to work from home or whose family situation limits his or her ability to travel might be interested in online professional service opportunities commonly referred to as virtual volunteering. Experts suggest that while virtual volunteering is not in widespread use, its potential for engaging some kinds of volunteers more effectively is enormous (Murray and Harrison 2005). At the conclusion of this chapter, we will offer further concrete suggestions on how to accommodate professional and personal life changes within a volunteer program.

Ultimately, we suggest with our examination of volunteering through life stages that larger matters are at stake. As we observed in Exhibit 3.23, fewer association volunteers in our sample express an interest in continued volunteering than those who intend to leave. This chapter will help us to understand how generational and life stage differences in our sample—a

> **"People at different life stages vary in motivations and capacities for volunteering."**
> – Fengyan Tang, 2006

key factor in volunteering behavior—might influence their intention to volunteer.

Understanding how age and career differences among your members influence their attitudes about association activity is about much more than their volunteering behavior. It is also about their likelihood of renewing membership in your association and encouraging their peers to join. A member who perceives insufficient value in membership is unlikely to volunteer, and vice versa. As a spate of articles tell us, younger and older association members can have quite different and unexpected perspectives about the value of association benefits. In an article in *Association Management,* published by the American Society of Association Executives, Jeffrey Cufaude reminded us as far back as 2000 that the operating practices many take for granted can frustrate younger members. And older members in leadership positions can overlook (or even cause) the real and perceived barriers that prevent younger members from assuming leadership positions.

We look to our data on association volunteering to answer the following questions: Among association volunteers, how will age and career level influence a member's choice and amount of volunteer activity, satisfaction with the outcomes, and expectations regarding appropriate recognition and support of their service? Further, if "people at different life stages vary in motivations and capacities for volunteering," their preferences and patterns of volunteer behavior should also be evident in their professional volunteering (Tang 2006, page 377). In this particular context, we might also consider these questions: What happens to association members near the point of retirement with respect to their intention to continue volunteering professionally? How do age and career level influence the reasons that volunteers offer for entering or departing volunteer activity, and what can associations do about the reasons? In THE DECISION TO JOIN, members who were compared across age groups reflected slightly (but not enormously) different attitudes toward associations, the benefits they associated with membership, and the ways they chose to engage in membership activities. In our comparison, we expected to find that volunteer activity is largely a reflection of age and, to a slighter extent, career level.

We compare association volunteers and non-volunteers across five age groups (Exhibit 5.1):

- Those born before 1945 (the Pre-war cohort)
- Those born between 1946 and 1954 (Early Boom)
- Those born between 1955 and 1962 (Late Boom)
- Those born between 1963 and 1976 (Gen X)
- Those born after 1977 (Millennials).

The majority of our respondents come from the middle three of these age groups, ranging in age from 32 to 62. The average respondent is 49 years old. We also compare survey responses across career level (shown in Exhibit 5.2).

EXHIBIT 5.1

Age

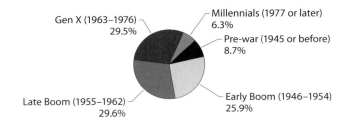

EXHIBIT 5.2

Career Situation (If Employed Outside Academia)

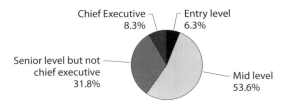

Exhibit 5.3 shows how age and career level intersect. About half of our survey respondents are in the middle level of their career path, while one third are at the senior level. The differences in career path among age levels are most evident with the Millennials, who are most likely to be at the entry level professionally.

EXHIBIT 5.3

Current Career Situation by Age

	Pre-war (1945 or before)	Early Boom (1946–1954)	Late Boom (1955–1962)	Gen X (1963–1976)	Millennials (1977 or later)
	%	%	%	%	%
Entry level	0.9	2.1	2.8	5.8	37.7
Mid level	27.6	45.9	52.2	62.7	56.3
Senior level but not chief executive	45.9	40.3	36.1	26.2	5.0
Chief executive	25.6	11.6	8.9	5.3	1.1

Influence of Age and Career Level on All Volunteering

How do age and career level influence volunteer patterns—first, in all organizations and, next, in cosponsoring organizations? Exhibit 5.4 shows that the youngest age groups are the least likely to be involved in volunteering for any organization (community-based or professional). Since age largely drives career level, we find a similar pattern in Exhibit 5.5, where those respondents at the highest career levels are most likely to be involved in volunteering.

Even so, across the age groups, our sample of association members represents individuals who are much more heavily involved in volunteering than national averages. Just five percent of Boomers and older age groups report that they have never volunteered for any organization; this figure increases to just 11–14 percent for younger age groups. As noted earlier,

EXHIBIT 5.4

Volunteering for Any Organization by Age

	Pre-war (1945 or before)	Early Boom (1946–1954)	Late Boom (1955–1962)	Gen X (1963–1976)	Millennials (1977 or later)
	%	%	%	%	%
In the last 12 months	81.9	79.6	82.1	71.8	62.1
In the past but not in the last 12 months	12.9	14.8	12.3	16.8	23.6
Never volunteered	5.2	5.6	5.6	11.4	14.3

the difference between our sample and national samples is most likely due to selection bias. We expect our sample captured more of the active volunteers than do other national studies.

Exhibit 5.6 reminds us that volunteerism can be supported by family habits. Across many studies, those who volunteer are much more likely to belong to families where family members volunteer. We can view this pattern as self-supporting: Younger generations might be more likely to enter volunteering where they have family role models, while older generations are most likely providing the role models to younger family members.

EXHIBIT 5.5

Volunteering for Any Organization by Career Level*

	Chief Executive	Senior level but not Chief Executive	Mid level	Entry level
	%	%	%	%
In the last 12 months	86.7	77.6	72.8	59.7
In the past but not in the last 12 months	9.4	14.6	17.3	25.9
Never volunteered	3.9	7.8	9.9	14.3

*For all tables displaying respondents by career level, only those who are currently employed in private industry, nonprofits, or government are included. These tables exclude business owners, academics, and the unemployed or retired, since career level is more difficult to describe for these groups. Because we exclude a good portion of our respondents from these tables, we use this level of comparison selectively and caution readers about the conclusions that can be made.

EXHIBIT 5.6

Does at least one other member of your immediate family (parents, siblings, spouse, or children) currently engage in volunteer activity or have they done so in the past?

	Pre-war (1945 or before)	Early Boom (1946–1954)	Late Boom (1955–1962)	Gen X (1963–1976)	Millennials (1977 or later)
	%	%	%	%	%
Yes	82.3	80.8	83.1	75.0	70.0
No	15.1	16.8	15.7	23.4	27.8
Not applicable/no immediate family members	2.7	2.3	1.2	1.7	2.3

In our sample, four out of five respondents report that at least one other family member volunteers. There could be some cause for concern in that the youngest age groups have the lowest affirmative response to this question. If this response indicates that younger association members have slightly weaker family connections to volunteering, organizations might consider stronger efforts to socialize the younger professionals into volunteer tasks and responsibilities.

Exhibits 5.7 and 5.8 show the number of organizations for which respondents volunteer and the types of activities in which they are engaged. These tables reflect only the current volunteers in our sample. In the first two tables, we see the same pattern as before, whereby an increase in age also increases the quantity of service a volunteer performs. The oldest volunteers perform the greatest hours of service to the most organizations.

EXHIBIT 5.7

For how many different organizations did you perform volunteer work in the last 12 months?

	Pre-war (1945 or before)	Early Boom (1946–1954)	Late Boom (1955–1962)	Gen X (1963–1976)	Millennials (1977 or later)
	%	%	%	%	%
One	17.2	17.8	16.2	20.4	31.5
Two	27.3	30.6	30.0	34.1	35.7
Three	27.5	28.8	29.9	27.3	21.7
Four	15.0	13.3	13.6	11.0	5.8
Five or more	12.9	9.6	10.3	7.2	5.2

The next table is useful for understanding volunteer preferences and how these might vary by age and family situation. In Exhibit 5.8, we observe a complex association between age and activity preference. As expected, older volunteers, given their greater knowledge, are most heavily involved in the professionally related activities. The younger cohorts display a preference for arts and creative activities, and for coaching/teaching (the latter likely due to their children's activities). The middle age cohort (Boomers) is most heavily relied on for fundraising, direct service, and organizing. Younger

EXHIBIT 5.8

Which of the following best describes the volunteer activities you performed for organizations in the past 12 months?

Respondents checked all applicable. Shown in percent of respondents who volunteer for any organization.

	Pre-war (1945 or before)		Early Boom (1946–1954)		Late Boom (1955–1962)		Gen X (1963–1976)		Millennials (1977 or later)	
	%	Rank	%	Rank	%	Rank	%	Rank	%	Rank
Direct service (e.g. preparing, serving, or delivering food, ushering, etc.)	41.7	2	44.9	2	47.9	2	41.0	3	44.6	1
Coach, referee, tutor, teacher, or mentor	27.4	5	33.4	5	43.2	3	49.0	2	41.5	2
Organizing groups and/or meetings	38.3	3	40.6	3	41.6	5	39.2	4	38.0	3
Serving on board(s) or committee(s)	68.7	1	63.3	1	59.0	1	50.1	1	34.1	4
Fundraising or selling items to raise money	35.0	4	37.1	4	42.0	4	38.8	5	28.8	5
Organizing promotional campaigns for events or other activities	14.8	10	13.6	10	13.7	9	12.9	7	15.4	6
Arts or creative activities	12.2	11	12.3	11	12.8	10	12.6	8	15.1	7
Working at a trade show, conference, or other meeting	19.9	8	19.2	6	17.0	6	14.7	6	14.5	8
Writing or presenting paper(s) or research reports at conferences or workshops	22.6	6	17.7	7	14.3	7	12.5	9	8.7	9
Providing counseling, medical care, fire/EMS, or protective services	16.9	9	13.6	9	11.3	11	10.0	11	7.0	10
Setting professional or industry standards or providing technical input	21.0	7	17.7	8	13.8	8	11.5	10	6.4	11
Presenting or testifying on behalf of any organization to any legislative body (local, state, federal, or global advocacy)	9.1	12	6.6	12	4.5	12	3.8	12	2.2	12

age groups are substantially less likely to serve on boards and committees. While these preferences may or may not translate directly into activities that your association offers its volunteers, they should help in giving you some direction about how to tailor your volunteer activities to appeal to the various generations in your membership.

Volunteering for Career-Related Reasons

In our comparison of volunteer behavior across age groups, particularly as it relates to professional volunteering, we would expect to find that younger volunteers are more attuned to the career benefits of volunteering. We look at this connection below, both in terms of the relationship between age and career objectives and that of career path and career objectives.

First, Exhibit 5.9 illustrates that those respondents at higher professional levels are more likely to report that they actively seek opportunities to contribute to their workplace skills through volunteering. At the senior and CEO levels, 75 percent of respondents agree that they do, compared to 62.6 percent at the entry level. The lesson for associations is that older professionals are most interested in passing on their expertise and knowledge, and this can often be accomplished through volunteering. Even so, while the motivation to connect volunteering and professional skill development increases with seniority, it is strong across all career levels. This interest by entry-level professionals in connecting volunteering to their professional activities should encourage association professionals to find more ways to engage even the least experienced in professional volunteering.

In comparing respondents by age and career level, we also find little difference between the least senior and most senior professionals in terms of the effect they perceive volunteering has had on their careers (Exhibit 5.10). About 90 percent of the most senior professionals report that volunteering has had a positive effect on their career (rating 4 or 5 on the 5-point scale), decreasing to 81.7 percent for the least senior professionals. The results do not vary across age groups but only across career levels (not shown). This result is important to note because we might find that entry-level professionals are reluctant to volunteer out of concern that it will conflict with work responsibilities. Rather, we find them slightly more ambivalent than older cohorts about the impact but generally positive about the opportunity.

We conclude from this analysis that it takes time for volunteers to understand the effects of volunteerism on their careers. At the outset, they may be both more enthusiastic about volunteering but also more uncertain about the career benefits of volunteering. We see this delayed effect in the response of one of our survey respondents, "After 10 years of volunteering with [a cosponsor organization] I have learned skills that have increased my career opportunities. Thank you for the opportunity to serve. I would love to be asked to serve again in the future."

Influence of Age and Career Level on Cosponsor Volunteering

Exhibit 5.11 displays the activities that survey respondents are performing for their associations. Keeping in mind as you read this that the older volunteers generally perform more hours of service for the cosponsor association, this table suggests that more activities are being performed by older volunteers than by younger groups. The difference is least pronounced for board and committee work and most pronounced for activities that demand technical or professional expertise.

Exhibits 5.12 and 5.13 display the levels and activities in which survey respondents volunteer for a cosponsoring organization. The majority of our respondents are not volunteering for their association even though they are involved in other community-based volunteering. An average of two thirds of respondents (highest at youngest ages and entry level) are not volunteering for their association. However, according to Exhibit 5.14 and 5.15, up to one fifth of the non-volunteer members have volunteered for the cosponsor in the past. Among those who do volunteer, most are involved in ad hoc volunteer activities (defined as a range of intermittent activities that occur outside of formal committee and board roles, such as membership recruitment, fundraising, etc.).

The preference of association members for community-based service over professional service is quite pronounced when Exhibit 5.16 is examined. This table compares, by age group, the number of hours respondents report contributing to all organizations against the number of hours they contribute to their cosponsor organization. Respondents are included only if they volunteer for either group. The results indicate that most volunteers are performing few hours of service for their cosponsor organization with little difference across age groups.

EXHIBIT 5.9

When you volunteer, do you actively seek opportunities to contribute your workplace skills?

	Chief Executive	Senior level but not Chief Executive	Mid level	Entry level
	%	%	%	%
Yes	75.5	75.3	68.7	62.6
No	24.5	24.7	31.3	37.4

EXHIBIT 5.10

What effect do you think volunteering has had on your career or, if you are self-employed, on your business?

	Chief Executive	Senior level but not Chief Executive	Mid level	Entry level
	%	%	%	%
Very negative	0.2	0.0	0.1	0.3
2	0.6	0.8	1.0	1.1
3	9.5	16.3	17.9	17.0
4	24.0	29.9	33.5	32.2
Very positive	65.6	53.0	47.5	49.5

EXHIBIT 5.11

In the last 12 months, have you done any of the following as a volunteer (in person, online, or in any other way) on behalf of [cosponsor]?
Respondent checked all applicable.

	Pre-war (1945 or before)		Early Boom (1946–1954)		Late Boom (1955–1962)		Gen X (1963–1976)		Millennials (1977 or later)	
	%	Rank	%	Rank	%	Rank	%	Rank	%	Rank
Recruited a member or members	13.6	3	14.7	3	12.5	3	10.6	2	9.4	1
Served on a committee for a local chapter or section	12.0	6	13.5	4	10.5	4	9.4	3	9.1	2
Provided mentoring, coaching, or tutoring for members, students, or others	20.5	2	17.2	2	14.2	1	11.4	1	9.0	3
Provided professional advice	22.9	1	17.3	1	12.6	2	9.3	4	6.5	4
Served on the board for a local chapter or section	7.5	11	9.2	7	7.2	7	5.9	7	6.0	5
Participated in a discussion group, expert panel, or report	13.6	4	10.7	6	8.2	5	7.1	6	5.0	6
Spoke or presented a paper	12.9	5	10.8	5	8.1	6	7.5	5	4.1	7
Raised funds	7.0	14	7.0	9	6.2	9	4.8	11	4.1	8
Moderated or facilitated discussion groups at meetings or elsewhere	9.1	8	8.1	8	6.5	8	4.9	10	2.6	9
Submitted a paper or manuscript for publication	7.4	12	5.4	14	4.2	14	5.3	9	2.4	10
Reviewed a paper or proposal for a publication	9.9	7	6.8	10	4.8	10	5.5	8	2.3	11
Reviewed proposals for conferences or projects	6.6	16	5.6	13	4.3	13	3.9	12	1.8	12
Reviewed research, conducted literature review, or resource reviews, or analyzed data	7.5	10	5.0	15	3.9	15	3.5	13	1.6	13
Served on a technical committee or reviewed standards and practices	7.3	13	5.8	12	4.6	11	3.2	14	1.6	14
Wrote proposals, grant applications, or business plans	4.5	17	3.3	17	2.3	17	2.7	16	1.6	15
Served on a committee for the parent organization	8.0	9	6.1	11	4.5	12	3.1	15	1.3	16
Reviewed applications as part of accreditation, certification, or competitive program	6.7	15	4.2	16	2.9	16	1.9	17	1.2	17
Made a presentation or testified on behalf of the organization to any legislative body (local, state, national, or global advocacy)	4.1	18	3.1	18	2.2	18	1.5	18	1.2	18
Prepared background for regulators, the press, or others	3.3	19	2.0	19	1.3	20	1.0	19	0.7	19
Served on the board for the parent organization	3.1	20	2.0	20	1.5	19	0.9	20	0.5	20

Exhibit 5.17 compares respondents by age group on the questions related to the Volunteer Functions Inventory (VFI). We also compare VFI questions related to community volunteering with those related to cosponsor volunteering. We would expect to find that respondents assign different value to the potential benefits of volunteering as they age and acquire professional skills. In particular, we expect that the career-related benefits of

EXHIBIT 5.12

Cosponsor Level of Volunteering by Age

	Pre-war (1945 or before)	Early Boom (1946–1954)	Late Boom (1955–1962)	Gen X (1963–1976)	Millennials (1977 or later)
	%	%	%	%	%
Governance	9.5	10.5	8.0	6.5	6.2
Committee/ongoing	12.3	11.2	9.0	8.1	5.7
Ad hoc	25.2	20.0	18.4	17.3	14.3
None	53.0	58.3	64.6	68.1	73.8

EXHIBIT 5.13

Cosponsor Level of Volunteering by Career Level

	Chief Executive	Senior level but not Chief Executive	Mid level	Entry level
	%	%	%	%
Governance	10.5	7.4	6.5	5.1
Committee/ongoing	7.8	10.0	7.7	6.1
Ad hoc	20.7	17.4	17.0	13.4
None	60.9	65.2	68.8	75.4

EXHIBIT 5.14

Have you ever volunteered for [cosponsor] in the past?

Asked only of respondents who have not volunteered for the cosponsor in the last 12 months.

	Pre-war (1945 or before)	Early Boom (1946–1954)	Late Boom (1955–1962)	Gen X (1963–1976)	Millennials (1977 or later)
	%	%	%	%	%
Yes	31.9	19.1	12.4	8.2	7.5
No	68.1	80.9	87.6	91.8	92.5

EXHIBIT 5.15

If yes: How long ago was that?

Asked only of respondents who have answered yes to the question shown in Exhibit 5.14.

	Pre-war (1945 or before)	Early Boom (1946–1954)	Late Boom (1955–1962)	Gen X (1963–1976)	Millennials (1977 or later)
	%	%	%	%	%
1–2 years ago	7.1	8.8	15.2	21.0	29.9
3–5 years ago	16.7	25.3	26.4	39.8	52.2
5–10 years ago	25.2	35.0	34.3	23.8	17.9
More than 10 years ago	51.1	30.9	24.2	15.4	0.0

EXHIBIT 5.16

On average, how many hours did you perform volunteer work in the last 12 months?

Asked only of respondents who have volunteered at the level described in the last 12 months.

	Pre-war (1945 or before)		Early Boom (1946–1954)		Late Boom (1955–1962)		Gen X (1963–1976)		Millennials (1977 or later)	
	For any organization	For the cosponsor	For any organization	For the cosponsor	For any organization	For the cosponsor	For any organization	For the cosponsor	For any organization	For the cosponsor
	%	%	%	%	%	%	%	%	%	%
1–12 hours	8.2	54.0	11.6	56.3	10.7	57.2	14.1	59.0	23.0	57.9
13–49 hours	25.0	24.9	26.7	26.2	26.9	28.0	30.9	25.9	34.2	26.0
50–99 hours	24.1	12.7	25.0	11.1	26.2	9.2	25.4	9.5	19.4	10.0
100–249 hours	25.8	6.0	23.0	4.1	23.6	4.1	19.8	4.6	15.3	4.5
250–499 hours	8.8	1.5	8.7	1.6	8.0	1.0	6.6	0.8	4.8	0.6
500 or more hours	8.0	0.8	5.0	0.8	4.6	0.5	3.3	0.3	3.3	1.0

EXHIBIT 5.17

Volunteer Functions Inventory (VFI)*

Regardless of your previous volunteer experience, how important or accurate would the following statements be for you in doing volunteer work?

By Generation

VFI Dimensions		Pre-war (1945 or before)		Early Boom (1946–1954)		Late Boom (1955–1962)		Gen X (1963–1976)		Millennials (1977 or later)	
		Volunteering in general	Volunteering for cosponsor	Volunteering in general	Volunteering for cosponsor	Volunteering in general	Volunteering for cosponsor	Volunteering in general	Volunteering for cosponsor	Volunteering in general	Volunteering for cosponsor
		Mean	Mean	Mean	Mean	Mean	Mean	Mean	Mean	Mean	Mean
Values	I feel it is important to help others	4.28	3.81	4.36	3.87	4.43	3.91	4.39	3.95	4.38	3.94
	I can do something for a profession or cause that is important to me	4.14	3.96	4.16	3.96	4.14	3.93	4.08	3.94	4.06	3.93
	I feel compassion toward people in need	3.96	3.43	4.08	3.50	4.13	3.53	4.09	3.57	4.08	3.55
Understanding	Volunteering allows me to gain a new perspective on things	3.72	3.15	3.87	3.41	3.90	3.42	3.90	3.50	4.00	3.65
	I can explore my own strengths	3.08	2.81	3.35	3.18	3.41	3.29	3.50	3.38	3.78	3.61
	I can learn new skills through direct, hands-on experience	3.18	2.75	3.32	3.17	3.33	3.32	3.44	3.39	3.70	3.69
Enhancement	Volunteering makes me feel needed	3.14	2.55	3.22	2.71	3.21	2.75	3.14	2.79	3.19	2.95
	Volunteering brings me satisfaction or recognition that I do not get at work	2.85	2.27	3.10	2.61	3.16	2.74	3.14	2.78	3.30	3.09
Career	I can make new contacts that might help my business or career	2.30	2.07	2.57	2.70	2.64	3.00	2.86	3.25	3.23	3.58
	Volunteer experience looks good on my resume	1.94	1.80	2.25	2.35	2.33	2.58	2.50	2.77	2.94	3.20
	Volunteering helps me to explore different career options	1.79	1.66	2.13	2.21	2.19	2.46	2.37	3.64	2.72	3.06
	Volunteering gives a competitive advantage to my business	1.92	1.82	2.09	2.25	2.13	2.45	2.32	2.71	2.60	3.00
	Volunteering can help me get my foot in the door at a place where I would like to work	1.60	1.52	1.87	2.02	1.96	2.30	2.18	2.54	2.63	3.03
Social	Volunteering is important to the people I respect	3.37	2.99	3.33	3.05	3.28	3.09	3.26	3.13	3.34	3.35
Protective	Volunteering helps me deal with some of my own problems	2.09	1.72	2.23	1.97	2.27	2.11	2.38	2.25	2.59	2.60

*The VFI compares volunteers according to what they believe they gain through volunteer work. Mean shows the average rating on a 1–5 scale with 5=very important. The 15 questions were rated by respondents twice in the survey. First, all respondents were asked about "volunteering in general." Later in the survey, the same questions were asked of respondents who currently volunteer for the cosponsor OR who have volunteered for the cosponsor anytime in the past. Items are grouped according to the six underlying dimensions identified in the Volunteer Functions Inventory (see Bibliography: Clary, Snyder, and Stukas 1996).

volunteering will be most important to the youngest volunteers, who have the most to gain through connecting volunteer activity to professional objectives.

The results do indeed suggest that age is associated with the relative value to which respondents assign volunteering benefits. The youngest volunteers are most likely to agree with the career-related reasons for volunteering, and this connection holds true both for community-based volunteering and for association volunteering. The older the age group, the less likely they volunteer for career benefits.

We find a second and interesting connection between age and reasons for volunteering. In general, the younger the age, the more strongly a respondent will agree that *any* reason has importance. This association is very slight and sometimes insubstantial, but it carries across all age groups and all kinds of voluntary activity. In other words, no matter what the reason for volunteering, and no matter whether the volunteering is professional or not, the youngest respondents agreed more strongly than older respondents with the importance of volunteering. These results suggest that younger volunteers are more eager to achieve benefits from their service, regardless of the benefit or focus of their efforts. Other research confirms the strong philanthropic motivations of those from the Gen X and Millennial generations (Center on Philanthropy 2008).

> *No matter what the reason for volunteering, the youngest respondents agreed more strongly than older respondents with the importance of volunteering.*

Exhibit 5.18 displays respondents' answers to the question of how they were recruited into volunteering for their association. Some methods would appear to offer particularly important opportunities for recruiting certain age groups, especially younger volunteers. Somewhat surprisingly, although we might assume that younger members are more "wired" than older age groups, they are not any more likely to use a web site or online recruiting tool to join volunteer activities. Despite their affinity for online tools, younger members are similar to their older counterparts in preferring the direct approach. Given this fact, it is rather alarming to see that the younger age groups report being asked to volunteer less often: 7.5 percent

EXHIBIT 5.18

How did you first learn about the volunteer opportunities available to you through [cosponsor]?

Asked only of those who either currently volunteer for the cosponsor or who have volunteered for the cosponsor in the past.

	Pre-war (1945 or before)	Early Boom (1946–1954)	Late Boom (1955–1962)	Gen X (1963–1976)	Millennials (1977 or later)
	%	%	%	%	%
I don't recall	27.0	26.7	24.3	28.7	27.2
Through a local chapter or section	14.7	14.1	14.4	14.0	14.4
At a meeting, conference, or other event	14.1	14.0	13.2	13.0	10.7
I was asked by another volunteer	14.0	14.9	14.6	10.2	7.5
A staff member of the organization asked me to volunteer	7.5	9.0	10.1	8.1	10.4
I answered a call/ad for volunteers	6.1	5.1	5.4	4.8	2.9
Through my employer (current or past)	3.3	4.6	5.4	6.0	6.9
Through a professor or someone at my university or school	4.0	2.8	2.2	4.9	11.5
Through a posting on their web site	2.3	2.7	3.2	3.8	3.2
I contacted the organization and offered to volunteer	2.8	2.5	3.3	2.6	3.2
I saw an advertisement in the organization's magazine or other publication	2.3	2.5	2.0	2.1	1.9
Other way	1.7	1.2	1.8	1.8	0.3

of Millennials and 10.2 percent of Gen Xers were asked by other volunteers, compared to more than 14 percent of older groups. On the other hand, the younger cohorts are more likely to have been recruited by employers or professors: 18.4 percent of Millennials and 10.9 percent of Gen Xers, compared to 7–8 percent of older age groups. And as noted earlier, the most frequent response to the question was no recollection about the method of recruitment. No senior moments here; the lack of recollection is consistent across age groups.

> **Although we might assume that younger members are more "wired" than older age groups, they are no more likely to use a web site or online recruiting tool to join volunteer activities.**

Satisfaction With Volunteering

When comparing levels of satisfaction with volunteering for the cosponsor organization, we find only slight differences across age groups. Generally, we find as we did earlier that volunteers are a pretty happy group across cohorts. However, older cohorts are more likely to have definite opinions either for or against volunteering for their cosponsor. They are both more likely to be dissatisfied and more likely to be satisfied (Exhibit 5.19). Younger cohorts, on the other hand, are slightly more likely to be ambivalent, indicated by a response of "3" on our five-point scale.

EXHIBIT 5.19

Please use the scale provided below to rate your overall satisfaction with volunteering for [cosponsor].
Asked only of those who have volunteered for the cosponsor.

	Pre-war (1945 or before)	Early Boom (1946–1954)	Late Boom (1955–1962)	Gen X (1963–1976)	Millennials (1977 or later)
	%	%	%	%	%
Very dissatisfied	1.9	2.0	1.7	1.5	0.8
2	7.2	7.7	6.9	4.8	4.5
3	33.8	35.3	37.0	37.1	37.3
4	36.2	35.6	35.4	38.3	41.7
Very satisfied	20.9	19.4	19.0	18.3	15.7

Younger respondents are more likely to anticipate volunteering for the cosponsor in the next 12 months but again with some ambivalence, as indicated by their strong response to the middle "3" on our scale (Exhibit 5.20). More than half (57.9 percent) of the pre-war volunteers indicate they are unlikely to volunteer. Half of the Boomers indicate they are unlikely to volunteer, while about one quarter report the opposite. About one quarter of Gen Xers and slightly more Millennials indicate that they are likely to volunteer.

EXHIBIT 5.20

How likely is it that you will be a volunteer for [cosponsor] within the next 12 months?
Asked of all respondents.

	Pre-war (1945 or before)	Early Boom (1946–1954)	Late Boom (1955–1962)	Gen X (1963–1976)	Millennials (1977 or later)
	%	%	%	%	%
Very unlikely	37.7	30.7	29.3	23.7	17.2
2	20.2	20.4	22.0	21.3	21.5
3	18.5	22.9	24.8	28.4	31.9
4	10.9	11.8	11.2	12.9	15.6
Very likely	12.8	14.1	12.6	13.8	13.9

On the question of whether they would recommend volunteering to a friend or colleague, the results are more closely balanced, with just slightly fewer respondents across the generations indicating that they would when compared to those who would not (Exhibit 5.21). We find an interesting middle dip here in that Late Boomers, our central age cohort, is least likely to recommend volunteering to others (29 percent would and 40 percent would not). We also find that about 30 percent of the younger cohorts would be likely to recommend volunteering for the cosponsor to a friend or colleague.

These results should concern association professionals. The youngest age group is less actively involved in recruiting its peers or being recruited by peers. Although it is to be expected that some older volunteers will phase out of the volunteering activities that are related to their professions

> *Averaging across the generations, for every one respondent who plans to continue volunteering, two respondents plan to leave and one more is ambivalent.*

as they retire, the proportion of younger volunteers indicating that they will continue to volunteer is not sufficient to replace the retirees. Put more bluntly, averaging across the generations, for every one respondent who plans to continue volunteering, two respondents plan to leave, and one more is ambivalent. Depending on the age group, up to 10 percent more respondents say they would not recommend volunteering to others than those who say they would. The solution to meeting future needs for association volunteers will lie equally in supporting the existing volunteers with effective resources and services and in recruiting new volunteers into association work.

Demographic Patterns

Exhibits 5.22 and 5.23 compare the age groups of survey respondents against gender and racial differences. The results in Exhibit 5.23 suggest a steady increase in the racial diversity of the average association's volunteer base as its membership gets younger. However, we do not see a clear pattern with gender: Association volunteers in younger age groups are more equally balanced than those in the oldest age group but are not much different from Boomers in terms of the mix of males and females. For associations with an explicit strategy to diversify their membership—culturally, racially, or by gender—volunteering patterns would appear to support greater efforts at diversification and diversity management. We also observe from Exhibit 5.24 that the younger the age group the more likely the respondent is to be based outside the United States.

EXHIBIT 5.21

How likely is it that you would recommend volunteering for [cosponsor] to a friend or colleague?

Asked of all respondents.

	Pre-war (1945 or before)	Early Boom (1946–1954)	Late Boom (1955–1962)	Gen X (1963–1976)	Millennials (1977 or later)
	%	%	%	%	%
Very unlikely	20.3	20.3	21.3	17.8	15.2
2	15.5	17.2	18.7	19.0	19.5
3	25.4	29.7	31.0	32.4	33.7
4	21.6	17.7	16.1	17.7	19.1
Very likely	17.2	15.1	12.9	13.2	12.5

EXHIBIT 5.22

Gender by Generation

	Pre-war (1945 or before)	Early Boom (1946–1954)	Late Boom (1955–1962)	Gen X (1963–1976)	Millennials (1977 or later)
	%	%	%	%	%
Male	66.0	54.1	52.9	60.9	55.1
Female	34.0	45.9	47.1	39.1	44.9

EXHIBIT 5.23

Race (US-based survey respondents only) by Generation

	Pre-war (1945 or before)	Early Boom (1946–1954)	Late Boom (1955–1962)	Gen X (1963–1976)	Millennials (1977 or later)
	%	%	%	%	%
White non-Hispanic	92.5	91.7	90.3	84.0	81.6
Other races and cultures	7.5	8.3	9.7	16.0	18.4

EXHIBIT 5.24

World Location by Generation

	Pre-war (1945 or before)	Early Boom (1946–1954)	Late Boom (1955–1962)	Gen X (1963–1976)	Millennials (1977 or later)
	%	%	%	%	%
United States	93.2	92.4	91.3	85.0	80.6
Outside United States	6.8	7.6	8.7	15.0	19.4

Age and Career: Key Implications

With respect to age and career paths, our study is different from other national studies of volunteering, where the objective of much of the inter-generational research has been on how to encourage people to volunteer in the first place. This national objective forms the basis of much public policy and makes sense when we understand how important family upbringing is to developing volunteerism. Rather, our comparison of association members across age groups is largely a study of different volunteering patterns across the generations. That is because our sample of association members represents individuals who are much more heavily involved in volunteering than national averages. Just 5 percent of Boomers and older age groups and just 11–14 percent of the younger members in our sample report that they have never volunteered, a smaller percentage than more representative U.S. samples.

> *"I've volunteered most of my life. It is something that is engrained in me. My grandparents taught me at a young age to pay it forward."*
>
> **– Association member**

This fact emphasizes that our analysis focuses more on how age and career path might influence the nature of a volunteer's public service rather than on how to create new volunteers. Associations looking to benefit from our research will take heart in knowing that the younger members of our sample are already strongly oriented toward civic service. Their socialization toward professional voluntary service may still be in the works, but

the hardest work has already been done (by their families, parents, schools, friends, etc.).

With an understanding that our study is different in this respect, we learn some important things about the age differences within our sample. First, it is striking that the differences across generations are subtle. There are no clear lines of demarcation between the attitudes of the old and young toward volunteering, but rather small degrees of difference. The second conclusion is that the differences between older and younger members are multi-dimensional and multi-directional. In some respects, older respondents are more positive about volunteering; in other respects, the greater enthusiasm comes from the youngest cohort. And somewhat surprisingly, at times the most negative responses come from neither the oldest nor the youngest. Age and career level matter when it comes to volunteering but not always in the expected ways. Following are the key generational differences, but keep in mind that some of these differences may be quite subtle.

First, this study suggests the following about older respondents:

- Older volunteers perform the greatest hours of service to the most organizations.
- They are most likely to come from families that volunteer.
- They are less likely to volunteer for career benefits.
- They are more likely to have definite opinions either for or against volunteering for their cosponsor.

Younger respondents are:

- More internationally and racially diverse.
- Less likely to be involved in any kind of volunteering or to come from families that volunteer.
- Less likely, particularly at the professional entry level, to be volunteering for their association.
- Less likely to have been asked to volunteer.
- More likely to indicate they will continue to volunteer for their association, and also the most likely to see benefits in volunteering.
- Less actively involved in recruiting their peers or being recruited by peers. We also observe that the proportion of younger volunteers

indicating that they will continue to volunteer is not sufficient to replace the retirees.

Consider this practical suggestion to take advantage of age and career differences in experience, motivations, activity preferences, and other variations in your volunteer ranks: Volunteerism can be viewed in your organization as something that follows a career path. Most volunteers of any kind expect to be given opportunities to transition to new kinds of challenges, and you can take advantage of this expectation by offering your volunteers opportunities that parallel their experience and seniority.

We also suggest that you consider how volunteers can support one another in their work—either across generations or within the same age group. Formal peer-to-peer matching and mentoring programs can be used to socialize new and younger volunteers or to involve older board and committee members in training new volunteers. Volunteers at all age levels can use the social networking skills appropriate to their generation to recruit others into professional volunteering. Associations wishing to involve younger professionals in volunteering should also be attuned to the messages that they send. One of our younger respondents attempted to explain why she was not involved in association volunteering: "The committees tend to be very 'old-school' and 'boys club' and difficult to break through as a younger member."

Market research on your volunteer cohorts can tell you what volunteer jobs appeal to various age groups, what kind of life-work balance they expect, and how to engage them in ways that make sense to them. Building flexibility into the volunteer program can foster long-term retention of volunteers by helping to accommodate them during transitions in their professional and family responsibilities. Encouraging staff to maintain a positive attitude about volunteers who come and go can also help retention, by reinforcing the value of keeping in touch with volunteers who temporarily leave your ranks due to job changes and family demands.

Above all, this analysis tells us not to make assumptions about the relationship between age and volunteering. One common assumption in volunteer management is that volunteers will perform the task that is handed to them—and will keep on doing it until they retire. Such an assumption is likely to lead to burnout and turnover in your volunteer ranks. What volunteers expect—especially long-term volunteers—is task variation and assignments appropriate to their skills (and skills change with time).

It may take more organizational effort to involve younger volunteers, but this study suggests that the results could be worthwhile given the enthusiasm they bring to the work.

A second assumption is that younger volunteers have less to offer. This kind of perspective on young volunteers—especially when expressed by the staff who work with volunteers—is equally likely to increase turnover in your volunteer ranks. It may take more organizational effort to involve younger volunteers, but this study suggests that the results could be worthwhile given the enthusiasm that they bring to the work.

A third assumption is that age and seniority will have the same effect on all volunteers. While we have aggregated our responses in this study, there are differences within the ranks alongside the commonalities. Take as an example the assumption that members who retire will also leave their professional volunteering behind. We offer two contrasting quotes from our survey to illustrate the variation in member attitudes. One respondent, who clearly intends to follow this path, told us, "After turning 50, I decided to focus on my underlying personal passions in life and not on career development as much. I've done what I should; now it's time for me to do what I love." But another member wrote, "Although I am currently retired, I may work part time in the future. My volunteer work with the local section provides an active professional connection." So, we see two volunteers from among the older ranks with quite different plans in mind about how they will connect their future volunteering to their professional world.

ACTING ON THE FINDINGS

Generations and Career Level

As this chapter suggests, having a clear understanding of the differences in age and career level among your members should inform your volunteer strategy. Consider using the tool that follows to develop a framework for understanding how members' ages and career levels relate to their volunteer activities—accordingly, use the information to plan an effective recruitment and retention strategy for each group. The example below compares member ages and can be repeated for career levels.

Questions/Factors	Pre-war (1945 or before)	Early Boom (1946–1954)	Late Boom (1955–1962)	Gen X (1963–1976)	Millennials (1977 or later)
What are the primary motivations to volunteer?					
What types of volunteer roles are most desired?					
What is the preferred environment for volunteer activities?					
What types of time constraints exist?					
What are the unique barriers to volunteering?					
What are the general sources of dissatisfaction relating to the volunteer experience?					
Does diversity within the overall membership base match diversity within the volunteer ranks?					
In what ways does staff support and encourage volunteers?					

Impact on Motivation and Satisfaction

Volunteer motivations and resultant satisfaction with the volunteering experience vary by age and career level. Additionally the capacity to volunteer varies according to one's personal situation. Both of these factors mean that organizations wishing to capture the time and talent of members must offer flexibility of choice and organizational support to meet their volunteers' needs and expectations.

As one generation retires from association volunteering, the younger generations need to fill these vacancies. Some suggestions to address the dynamic nature of volunteering:

• Establish different volunteer opportunities that reflect the various life stages and preferences of your volunteers. Develop a career path of volunteering that meets your needs and your volunteers' needs over time. Target your recruitment efforts with different messages to address different life and professional stages.

• Identify opportunities for your volunteers to change course based upon their life course. Give your volunteers the opportunity to opt out but with an opportunity to volunteer again in the future.

• Communicate to your members that as a volunteer your association can meet their needs throughout their life course.

• This study suggests a strong connection between volunteerism and family upbringing, but not all of your members will share that background. Thinking especially of younger members, develop workplace messages and strategies with employers to enlist those members who have not been socialized into volunteering.

• Promote and highlight your volunteer opportunities in different ways to each generation and career level. Volunteer recruitment is not a one-size-fits-all proposition.

• Assess the attitudes of your volunteer and paid leadership. Do you encourage or enable members regardless of age to volunteer for particular tasks or committees, or are there hidden barriers to volunteering?

• A majority of members at all career levels actively seek volunteer opportunities to contribute their workplace skills. However, be aware that some volunteers may be tired of using their workplace skills in their volunteer activities (such as accountants who are asked to serve as treasurers).

- This study suggests that the proportion of younger volunteers is not sufficient to replace the retiring Boomers. Develop specific volunteer recruitment messages to target Gen X and Millennials to meet the future demand for volunteers. Develop other messages to encourage Boomers to volunteer in their professions post-retirement.

- Make sure you provide opportunities for younger members to move into leadership positions—and that those members are aware of those opportunities.

- One volunteer activity favored by all age groups was member recruitment. Compare your volunteer list against your member sponsor list to track this phenomenon in your association. How many of your new members are recruited by volunteers compared to other methods? Do the members your active volunteers recruit become volunteers themselves? Lastly, consider that if they are top member recruiters, they could be top volunteer recruiters as well—consider adding a volunteer sponsor line on your membership application.

CHAPTER **6**

Gender and Family Composition

MANY PERSONAL CHARACTERISTICS OF your members such as age, gender, race, and family composition, will influence their volunteering behavior. These characteristics influence societal expectations, volunteer motivations, and the kinds of volunteer opportunities available to people (Wilson and Musick 1997). To understand their influence, it is important to keep these personal characteristics in context. For example, as we explored in the previous chapter, how the age of your members relates to volunteering is less about their birthdate than it is about their experience, amount of time in the profession, and career level. This chapter will address age as it relates to life status: whether a member is married and has children. We also examine how a member's gender influences volunteer roles and satisfaction levels.

Gender and Volunteering

It is quite common in studies to find differences between men and women in their volunteer behavior; we reported some of these differences in Chapter 2. But what these differences signify is the more difficult question. Women often rate themselves as more altruistic than men on self-rating instruments (Wilson 2000). They also volunteer more. Should we then assume that women are more generous than men? Instead, perhaps the sexes manifest their generosity in different ways. Men and women are both socialized into helping behaviors, but differences in their upbringing and role expectations can create differences in how they manifest those behaviors through volunteering. These differences might explain, in turn, why some studies find men more likely to volunteer while others find the opposite, and still more find an indeterminate effect.

With the understanding that nurture may be more important than nature in explaining gender differences in volunteering, we summarize what past studies have concluded. First, on tests of the Volunteer Functions Inventory, gender influences both the strength and the rank ordering of the six motivational dimensions. Women tend to agree more strongly than men with the importance of volunteering for any reason. Both men and women rank functions related to values as the most important dimension, but men rank careers higher than women (Clary, Snyder, and Stukas 1996; Fletcher and Major 2004; Papadakis, Griffin, and Frater 2004). Second, to understand the influence of gender on volunteer tasks, Rotolo and Wilson (2007) used the Bureau of Labor Statistics data to find that men and women assume different volunteer roles. Men are more likely to teach, coach, serve on boards and committees, and perform maintenance work, while women are more likely to raise funds, serve food, and manage events. In other words, even after controlling for career and family status, men and women tend to prefer volunteer roles that are consistent with societal expectations.

Volunteering in the Family Life Cycle

Family roles are not fixed. Experts observe that motives of volunteers shift with age, marital, and parental status. Even after accounting for changes in their career paths, as volunteers proceed through personal stages in their life—getting married, raising children—their marital and parental status will influence their volunteer activity. In older research, Knoke and Thomson (1977) find that family life cycle influences the number of organizations to which individuals belong and the job-related nature of their volunteering activity. Somewhat surprisingly, when they examined memberships, they found that young couples with children belonged to as many organizations as those without.

Men and women are both socialized into helping behaviors, but differences in their upbringing and role expectations can create differences in how they manifest those behaviors through volunteering.

Professional and trade associations will share a particular concern that men and women might enter the labor force and commence career-related volunteer activities only to abandon them when family responsibilities intervene. Such a pattern would be inefficient and a source of frustration to associations that have to replace these volunteers. For men or women who assume the primary child-raising role (and we proceed here with the understanding that every family unit divides its responsibilities differently), the difference between whether they volunteer or not may depend on the ages of their children, and whether or not they continue to work. A job and family responsibilities can cause time pressures and reduce the time available for volunteering, but they can also offer a rationale and greater opportunities for volunteering.

Rotolo and Wilson (2007) suggest that a particularly important distinction regarding volunteer availability might be made between those parents with pre-school children (who are more occupied with their children and more socially isolated) and those with school-age children (who are more likely to volunteer for family-related activities). Although they suggest that children become an incentive rather than a barrier to volunteering, they do not distinguish between community volunteering and professional volunteering. In their analysis of BLS data, they find that full-time workers with school-age children actually volunteer more than those without children. Such results would be encouraging to association professionals looking to recruit volunteers from among their child-raising members.

Gender Distribution of Our Sample

As noted in Chapter 3, our sample was distributed unevenly between men and women: 56.6 percent of respondents are men and 43.4 percent are women. Distribution by marital status is also uneven. Men are more likely to be married or partnered than women in our sample (89.1 percent compared to 77.4 percent for women). Men are also more likely than women to have children at home (47 percent compared to 35 percent for women).

It is unclear how much age differences contribute to these gender differences: The mean and median respondent age is the same for men and women (age 49). However, Exhibit 6.1 suggests that the age distribution of the two genders is slightly different, with the ages of men dispersed across the five age cohorts more than women, who are concentrated in the Boom generations.

We found no differences between men and women on whether they have close family members who volunteer. But we did find that women in our sample were more likely to be employed part time than men (11.1 percent versus 3.1 percent) and less likely to be employed full time (83.8 percent of women versus 92.9 percent of men). In addition, 72.2 percent of women in our sample were at the entry- or mid-level of their careers, compared to 52.6 percent of men.

EXHIBIT 6.1

Generation by Gender

	Male	Female
	%	%
Pre-war (1945 or before)	10.1	6.9
Early Boom (1946–1954)	24.7	27.6
Late Boom (1955–1962)	27.5	32.3
Gen X (1963–1976)	31.6	26.7
Millennials (1977 or later)	6.1	6.6

With respect to the educational levels of our respondents, women are more likely to hold a bachelor's degree or less (51.3 percent compared to 44.7 percent of men). With the exception of medical degrees, women were slightly more likely than men to hold a master's or doctoral degree (44.6 percent of women and 41.1 percent of men). In our sample, 14.2 percent of men held a medical degree, compared to 4 percent of women.

For any of these various reasons, these results suggest that the differences between male and female responses in this study may be due to family and career status rather than gender.

The Influence of Gender on Volunteer Activity

When we examine volunteering levels, we find only a slight difference between men and women who currently volunteer or have volunteered in the past (Exhibit 6.2), although women are slightly more likely than men to report volunteering in the past year.

EXHIBIT 6.2

Volunteering for Any Organization by Gender

	Male	Female
	%	%
In the last 12 months	75.6	79.2
In the past but not in the last 12 months	15.5	14.6
Never volunteered	8.9	6.3

In terms of their choices of volunteer activity, men are substantially more involved in professional, technical and trade, public safety, sports and hobby, and cultural or arts organizations. Women are more likely to volunteer for hospitals, clinics, or other health organizations and for organizations focused on educational or youth service, environmental or animal care, and religious endeavors (Exhibit 6.3). Exhibit 6.4 suggests that men are more likely to be involved in setting professional or industry standards, writing or presenting papers, coaching and mentoring, and serving on boards or committees. Although board and committee service is the most frequent activity for the women in our sample, they appear to be more oriented toward organizing, creative, fundraising, and direct service activities. In other activities, men and women make similar choices. Thus, we appear to see some of the same pattern observed in previous research regarding gender roles and volunteering.

EXHIBIT 6.3

Which of the following best describes the type(s) of organizations for which you volunteered in the last 12 months? (Check all that apply.)

	Male	Female
	%	%
Civic, community service	48.2	47.0
Religious	44.0	46.7
Educational or youth service	39.6	42.8
Professional, technical, or trade	44.0	39.8
Sport, hobby, cultural, or arts	30.0	21.9
Nonprofit health organization other than a hospital or clinic	12.8	17.0
Hospital or clinic	7.4	10.4
Environmental or animal care	5.6	7.8
Political group or party	5.6	5.2
Public safety	5.4	2.6

EXHIBIT 6.4

Which of the following best describes the volunteer activities you performed for organization(s) in the past 12 months? (Check all that apply.)

	Male	Female
	%	%
Serving on board(s) or committee(s)	59.8	54.1
Direct service (e.g. preparing, serving, or delivering food, ushering, etc.)	40.6	49.1
Fundraising or selling items to raise money	34.0	43.9
Organizing groups and/or meetings	39.7	40.7
Coach, referee, tutor, teacher, or mentor	44.0	36.2
Working at a trade show, conference, or other meeting	15.4	19.2
Arts or creative activities	8.3	17.9
Organizing promotional campaigns for events or other activities	13.5	13.7
Writing or presenting paper(s) or research reports at conferences or workshops	16.7	13.5
Providing counseling, medical care, fire/EMS, or protective services	11.5	12.1
Setting professional or industry standards or providing technical input	17.4	11.1
Presenting or testifying on behalf of any organization to any legislative body (local, state, federal, or global advocacy)	5.7	4.4

Level of Participation in Volunteer Work

When we compare men and women on their level of participation in volunteer work, men report volunteering more hours on average than women (Exhibit 6.5). Regarding the number of organizations they serve (Exhibit 6.6), men are more likely than women to serve five or more organizations, but they are quite similar at lower levels of service.

EXHIBIT 6.5

Approximately how many total hours did you perform volunteer work for all the organizations you volunteered for in the last 12 months?

	Male	Female
	%	%
1–12 hours	10.1	14.8
13–49 hours	26.7	30.3
50–99 hours	25.5	24.6
100–249 hours	24.0	19.8
250–499 hours	8.6	6.6
500 or more hours	5.1	4.0

EXHIBIT 6.6

For how many different organizations did you perform volunteer work in the last 12 months?

	Male	Female
	%	%
One	19.0	18.5
Two	31.3	31.5
Three	27.5	29.3
Four	12.4	12.7
Five or more	10.0	8.1

The Influence of Marital and Family Status on Volunteer Activity

Viewed through the lens of marital and family status, the volunteering activity of respondents reflects a consistent pattern. Those who are married, who have children living at home full time, and who have immediate family members who volunteer are more likely to volunteer themselves (Exhibit 6.7). Other national studies also link volunteer activity to family status. The difference that family habits make is particularly evident in relation to family volunteer history, where individuals are much more likely to volunteer when they belong to families with a volunteer ethic.

Those respondents with children living at home full time are less likely to volunteer for professional, technical, or trade organizations or for civic or community service, environmental or animal care, political, and health

EXHIBIT 6.7

Have you performed any work as a volunteer through or for any organization?

	Marital/partner status		Children in household			Family volunteer history		
	Married/ partnered	Unmarried/ not partnered	Full time	Part of the time	No children	Other immediate family member volunteers	No other family member volunteers	Not applicable/ no immediate family members
	%	%	%	%	%	%	%	%
In the last 12 months	78.5	70.0	79.9	74.2	75.2	83.5	52.4	60.5
In the past but not in the last 12 months	14.3	19.1	12.3	16.7	17.2	12.8	24.2	20.8
Never volunteered	7.2	10.9	7.9	9.1	7.6	3.7	23.5	18.6

and public safety organizations. Instead, they volunteer for family-oriented organizations: youth agencies and religious, sports, or cultural organizations (Exhibit 6.8). The pattern appears to be influenced by the ages of children, since certain activities (civic, environmental, public safety) are preferred by those with older children living part time at home. Those without children at home gravitate toward professional, civic, and health activities. From our perspective, this pattern means that association members with children could be more difficult to recruit into professionally oriented volunteer activities.

The number of hours of service performed by respondents varied very little according to marital status or whether the respondent had family members who volunteer, or number of children in household (results not shown). However, the number of organizations the respondent volunteered for increased as family volunteering increased (Exhibit 6.9).

Those who are married, who have children living at home, and who have immediate family members who volunteer are more likely to volunteer themselves.

EXHIBIT 6.8

Which of the following best describes the type(s) of organizations for which you volunteered in the last 12 months? (Check all that apply.)

	Children in household		
	Full time	Part of the time	No children
	%	%	%
Professional, technical, or trade	38.4	44.3	44.8
Civic, community service	45.0	49.9	49.9
Educational or youth service	52.7	42.8	31.8
Environmental or animal care	4.8	11.4	7.7
Hospital or clinic	6.9	9.2	10.1
Nonprofit health organization other than a hospital or clinic	11.7	15.6	17.0
Political group or party	4.1	5.9	6.4
Public safety	3.6	6.4	4.5
Religious	50.3	38.8	41.4
Sport, hobby, cultural, or arts	36.1	24.8	18.8

EXHIBIT 6.9

For how many different organizations did you perform volunteer work in the last 12 months?

	Other immediate family member volunteers	No other family member volunteers	Not applicable/ no immediate family members
	%	%	%
One	16.7	31.5	26.3
Two	30.6	35.8	30.8
Three	29.3	22.4	24.6
Four	13.4	6.5	8.9
Five or more	9.9	3.9	9.4

Gender, Family Status, and the Motivation to Volunteer

We compared the influence of gender, marital/partner status, and family status on the reasons that individuals might volunteer. The Volunteer Functions Inventory is also compared on another dimension: We examined the reasons that respondents provide for their general volunteer activity against the reasons they might offer for association (cosponsor) volunteering. As we have already discovered in earlier analyses (see Chapter 3), when general volunteering is compared to cosponsor volunteering, our respondents are more likely to agree with the career-related benefits of volunteering with respect to their cosponsor volunteering, but otherwise they appear to derive more benefits from volunteering through community organizations.

Looking first at gender differences (Exhibit 6.10), we find that men and women rank the importance they place on each dimension in the same order. Those reasons related to promoting personal values through volunteering (Values) are ranked as most important, followed by reasons related to learning and exploring (Understanding), and so on. Both men and women ranked the career-related benefits of volunteering as relatively lower in importance. However, men and women differ in the relative level of importance they place on any reason for volunteering. Women are more likely, across all dimensions, to place greater importance on all reasons for volunteering. This result is consistent with the other studies cited earlier. It does not mean that women volunteer more, but they do appear to demonstrate greater enthusiasm about volunteering. This difference holds true for both general volunteering and cosponsor volunteering.

When marital/partner status (Exhibit 6.11) is compared, those respondents who are unmarried or unpartnered are more likely to agree with any reason for volunteering when compared to those who are married or partnered. This difference also holds true for both general volunteering and cosponsor volunteering. The differences, however, are quite slight and not substantial, and they disappear once we control for age and gender (results not shown).

When we compare the VFI responses of those with children at home to those without (Exhibit 6.12) we find that those with children are more likely to agree about the career-related importance of volunteering but only for cosponsor volunteering. We found no other differences across dimensions or family status. For easier interpretation, we have simplified the VFI comparisons by omitting some data. In Exhibit 6.12 we compare respondents with children at home full time to respondents with no children at home (omitting those with children at home part time).

On the question of whether immediate family members volunteered (Exhibit 6.13), we found an interesting pattern. As we might expect, family volunteering increased the importance of volunteering for both cosponsor and general volunteering but only for certain questions. Respondents who have immediate family members who volunteer are actually *less* likely to give importance to the career-related reasons for volunteering and also to reasons related to gaining perspective and new skills, feeling needed, and dealing with problems through volunteering. Those with family members who volunteer were likely to rate just one dimension as more important: the Values dimension. The results suggest that family volunteering helps to impart values about volunteering related to the more altruistic reasons for public service. Again, for easier interpretation we simplified this comparison, examining only immediate family members who volunteer to those with no family volunteering (omitting non-applicable responses from those with no immediate family members).

EXHIBIT 6.10

Volunteer Functions Inventory (VFI)*

Regardless of your previous volunteer experience, how important or accurate would the following statements be for you in doing volunteer work?

By Gender

VFI Dimensions		Male		Female	
		Volunteering in general	Volunteering for cosponsor	Volunteering in general	Volunteering for cosponsor
		Mean	Mean	Mean	Mean
Values	I feel it is important to help others	4.31	3.78	4.49	4.05
	I can do something for a profession or cause that is important to me	4.01	3.83	4.27	4.08
	I feel compassion toward people in need	3.95	3.35	4.27	3.76
Understanding	Volunteering allows me to gain a new perspective on things	3.78	3.29	4.01	3.57
	I can explore my own strengths	3.25	3.05	3.62	3.48
	I can learn new skills through direct, hands-on experience	3.23	3.08	3.56	3.45
Enhancement	Volunteering makes me feel needed	3.01	2.62	3.39	2.88
	Volunteering brings me satisfaction or recognition that I do not get at work	3.05	2.58	3.22	2.78
Career	I can make new contacts that might help my business or career	2.67	2.82	2.73	2.97
	Volunteer experience looks good on my resume	2.24	2.36	2.53	2.66
	Volunteering helps me to explore different career options	2.13	2.21	2.37	2.56
	Volunteering gives a competitive advantage to my business	2.19	2.38	2.17	2.43
	Volunteering can help me get my foot in the door at a place where I would like to work	1.91	2.10	2.14	2.36
Social	Volunteering is important to the people I respect	3.25	3.01	3.36	3.19
Protective	Volunteering helps me deal with some of my own problems	2.27	2.06	2.33	2.11

*The VFI compares volunteers according to what they believe they gain through volunteer work. Mean shows the average rating on a 1–5 scale with 5=very important. The 15 questions were rated by respondents twice in the survey. First, all respondents were asked about "volunteering in general." Later in the survey, the same questions were asked of respondents who currently volunteer for the cosponsor OR who have volunteered for the cosponsor anytime in the past. Items are grouped according to the six underlying dimensions identified in the Volunteer Functions Inventory (see Bibliography: Clary, Snyder, and Stukas 1996).

EXHIBIT 6.11

Volunteer Functions Inventory (VFI)*

Regardless of your previous volunteer experience, how important or accurate would the following statements be for you in doing volunteer work?

By Partner Status

VFI Dimensions		Married/ Partnered		Unmarried/ Unpartnered	
		Volunteering in general	Volunteering for cosponsor	Volunteering in general	Volunteering for cosponsor
		Mean	Mean	Mean	Mean
Values	I feel it is important to help others	4.39	3.89	4.37	3.94
	I can do something for a profession or cause that is important to me	4.12	3.93	4.14	3.97
	I feel compassion toward people in need	4.09	3.51	4.09	3.61
Understanding	Volunteering allows me to gain a new perspective on things	3.87	3.39	3.94	3.52
	I can explore my own strengths	3.39	3.21	3.57	3.41
	I can learn new skills through direct, hands-on experience	3.34	3.21	3.51	3.40
Enhancement	Volunteering makes me feel needed	3.17	2.72	3.24	2.82
	Volunteering brings me satisfaction or recognition that I do not get at work	3.11	2.64	3.21	2.83
Career	I can make new contacts that might help my business or career	2.66	2.86	2.85	2.97
	Volunteer experience looks good on my resume	2.33	2.47	2.55	2.62
	Volunteering helps me to explore different career options	2.18	2.33	2.46	2.54
	Volunteering gives a competitive advantage to my business	2.17	2.40	2.27	2.45
	Volunteering can help me get my foot in the door at a place where I would like to work	1.97	2.18	2.24	2.41
Social	Volunteering is important to the people I respect	3.30	3.09	3.28	3.08
Protective	Volunteering helps me deal with some of my own problems	2.26	2.05	2.45	2.24

* The VFI compares volunteers according to what they believe they gain through volunteer work. Mean shows the average rating on a 1–5 scale with 5=very important. The 15 questions were rated by respondents twice in the survey. First, all respondents were asked about "volunteering in general." Later in the survey, the same questions were asked of respondents who currently volunteer for the cosponsor OR who have volunteered for the cosponsor anytime in the past. Items are grouped according to the six underlying dimensions identified in the Volunteer Functions Inventory (see Bibliography: Clary, Snyder, and Stukas 1996).

EXHIBIT 6.12

Volunteer Functions Inventory (VFI)*

Regardless of your previous volunteer experience, how important or accurate would the following statements be for you in doing volunteer work?

By Children Under Age 18 in Household

VFI Dimensions		Children		No Children	
		Volunteering in general	Volunteering for cosponsor	Volunteering in general	Volunteering for cosponsor
		Mean	Mean	Mean	Mean
Values	I feel it is important to help others	4.43	3.91	4.36	3.90
	I can do something for a profession or cause that is important to me	4.10	3.91	4.14	3.96
	I feel compassion toward people in need	4.10	3.51	4.08	3.54
Understanding	Volunteering allows me to gain a new perspective on things	3.88	3.42	3.88	3.41
	I can explore my own strengths	3.40	3.28	3.43	3.22
	I can learn new skills through direct, hands-on experience	3.33	3.28	3.40	3.21
Enhancement	Volunteering makes me feel needed	3.15	2.74	3.20	2.74
	Volunteering brings me satisfaction or recognition that I do not get at work	3.14	2.71	3.11	2.65
Career	I can make new contacts that might help my business or career	2.70	3.06	2.68	2.76
	Volunteer experience looks good on my resume	2.37	2.63	2.36	2.41
	Volunteering helps me to explore different career options	2.21	2.50	2.24	2.28
	Volunteering gives a competitive advantage to my business	2.19	2.56	2.17	2.31
	Volunteering can help me get my foot in the door at a place where I would like to work	2.01	2.35	2.01	2.13
Social	Volunteering is important to the people I respect	3.30	3.10	3.30	3.08
Protective	Volunteering helps me deal with some of my own problems	2.29	2.13	2.29	2.05

* The VFI compares volunteers according to what they believe they gain through volunteer work. Mean shows the average rating on a 1–5 scale with 5=very important. The 15 questions were rated by respondents twice in the survey. First, all respondents were asked about "volunteering in general." Later in the survey, the same questions were asked of respondents who currently volunteer for the cosponsor OR who have volunteered for the cosponsor anytime in the past. Items are grouped according to the six underlying dimensions identified in the Volunteer Functions Inventory (see Bibliography: Clary, Snyder, and Stukas 1996).

EXHIBIT 6.13

Volunteer Functions Inventory (VFI)*

Regardless of your previous volunteer experience, how important or accurate would the following statements be for you in doing volunteer work?

By Immediate Family Volunteerism

VFI Dimensions		Family Volunteering		No Family Volunteering	
		Volunteering in general	Volunteering for cosponsor	Volunteering in general	Volunteering for cosponsor
		Mean	Mean	Mean	Mean
Values	I feel it is important to help others	4.44	3.92	4.17	3.80
	I can do something for a profession or cause that is important to me	4.17	3.97	3.93	3.82
	I feel compassion toward people in need	4.13	3.53	3.93	3.53
Understanding	Volunteering allows me to gain a new perspective on things	3.91	3.41	3.76	3.43
	I can explore my own strengths	3.41	3.23	3.44	3.29
	I can learn new skills through direct, hands-on experience	3.35	3.23	3.45	3.29
Enhancement	Volunteering makes me feel needed	3.18	2.71	3.17	2.84
	Volunteering brings me satisfaction or recognition that I do not get at work	3.12	2.64	3.12	2.79
Career	I can make new contacts that might help my business or career	2.64	2.87	2.89	2.93
	Volunteer experience looks good on my resume	2.31	2.46	2.57	2.62
	Volunteering helps me to explore different career options	2.15	2.32	2.52	2.54
	Volunteering gives a competitive advantage to my business	2.13	2.37	2.36	2.55
	Volunteering can help me get my foot in the door at a place where I would like to work	1.93	2.17	2.32	2.43
Social	Volunteering is important to the people I respect	3.32	3.09	3.19	3.06
Protective	Volunteering helps me deal with some of my own problems	2.25	2.03	2.45	2.29

*The VFI compares volunteers according to what they believe they gain through volunteer work. Mean shows the average rating on a 1–5 scale with 5=very important. The 15 questions were rated by respondents twice in the survey. First, all respondents were asked about "volunteering in general." Later in the survey, the same questions were asked of respondents who currently volunteer for the cosponsor OR who have volunteered for the cosponsor anytime in the past. Items are grouped according to the six underlying dimensions identified in the Volunteer Functions Inventory (see Bibliography: Clary, Snyder, and Stukas 1996).

So the pattern we have seen in other levels of analysis continues here as well. The reasons for volunteering that are most salient across demographic and career levels are related to acting on personal values of service and compassion. Gender is important mainly in influencing the sense of importance that volunteers bring to their service. One finding will be encouraging to associations: If those with children are more likely to agree about the career-related importance of volunteering, it may be possible to attract more members to professional volunteering during their child-raising years. Although parents are more likely to find that family-related volunteering competes for their time as professional volunteers, they nonetheless maintain a sense of the professional value of volunteering.

Volunteering for Career-Related Reasons

Associations will naturally be interested in whether any volunteer activity by members has career-related objectives or benefits. On gender, we find that women are more likely than men to assess the impact of volunteering on their career as a positive one (Exhibit 6.14). Overall, the gender difference is slight: 85.6 percent of women rate the effect of volunteering on their career as positive or very positive, compared to 83.2 percent of men. However, women are substantially more likely than men to assess the impact as very positive.

EXHIBIT 6.14

What effect do you think volunteering has had on your career or, if you are self-employed, on your business?

	Male	Female
	%	%
Very negative	0.2	0.1
2	1.0	0.7
3	16.6	13.6
4	32.4	26.4
Very positive	49.8	59.2

On family status and volunteering, we would expect to find that parents are less interested in applying their workplace skills to volunteering, because they are more focused on family volunteering. We do find such a relationship in that respondents with children at home are less likely to seek opportunities to contribute to workplace skills through volunteering than those without children at home (Exhibit 6.15). However, the difference is quite slight, and more than two thirds of the respondents who are actively raising children (69 percent) still report that they look for opportunities to connect volunteering to their profession. We suggest that the assumption that active parents are interested only in family-related volunteering activities is overstated. Rather, these results suggest that family activities compete with professional activities to some extent but that many volunteers still seek opportunities in both arenas.

EXHIBIT 6.15

When you volunteer do you ever actively seek opportunities to contribute your workplace skills?

	Children in household		
	Full time	Part of the time	No children
	%	%	%
Yes	69.0	72.5	74.4
No	31.0	27.5	25.6

Gender and Cosponsor Volunteering

A total of 35.4 percent of the men and 37.8 percent of the women in our sample have volunteered for the cosponsor in the past 12 months (not shown). An additional 7–10 percent of men and women have volunteered for their association in the past but not presently. However, men report that they volunteer more hours for their association than do women (Exhibit 6.16). A total of 18.1 percent of men contribute 50 or more hours per year, compared to 14.3 percent of women (50 hours is roughly the average number of hours that Americans contribute overall). Among both men and women, the average number of hours volunteered for association activities is quite low, particularly when compared to general volunteering.

EXHIBIT 6.16

On average, how many hours did you perform volunteer work for [cosponsor] in the last 12 months?

	Male	Female
	%	%
1–12 hours	54.4	60.5
13–49 hours	27.5	25.2
50–99 hours	10.9	9.3
100–249 hours	5.0	3.7
250–499 hours	1.4	0.9
500 or more hours	0.8	0.4

We also find that men and women perform slightly different kinds of activities for cosponsors (results not shown). Among the various volunteering activities included in our survey, men are more likely than women to have prepared background for regulators, served on the board or committee of a parent organization, submitted, reviewed or presented a paper, or developed grant proposals or business plans. Women were more likely than men to have served on the board or committee of a local chapter or section, mentored or coached a member, or raised funds for the organization. Women were also one third more likely to have recruited a member.

With respect to recruitment, women are more likely to have volunteered through a meeting or local chapter (Exhibit 6.17). Men are more likely to have been recruited into volunteering by another volunteer. With these exceptions, men and women otherwise learn about association volunteer activities in similar ways.

Gender and Satisfaction with Volunteering for Cosponsor

As we found previously, this section of our analysis once again demonstrates that women are more likely to emphasize the benefits of volunteering than are men. In Exhibit 6.18, we find that women were more satisfied than men about the specific aspects of their volunteer experience. Exhibits 6.19, 6.20, and 6.21 show that women are slightly more likely than men to find satisfaction with their association volunteering experience overall, intend

EXHIBIT 6.17

How did you first learn about the volunteer opportunities available to you through [cosponsor]?

Asked only of those who either currently volunteer for the cosponsor or who have volunteered for the cosponsor in the past.

	Male	Female
	%	%
I don't recall	28.5	24.1
Through a local chapter or section	13.1	15.8
At a meeting, conference, or other event	12.3	14.9
I was asked by another volunteer	14.4	11.8
A staff member of the organization asked me to volunteer	8.5	9.4
I answered a call/ad for volunteers	4.8	5.5
Through my employer (current or past)	4.8	5.4
Through a professor or someone at my university or school	3.8	3.5
Through a posting on their web site	2.7	3.5
I contacted the organization and offered to volunteer	3.3	2.2
I saw an advertisement in the organization's magazine or other publication	2.4	2.3

to volunteer in the future for the cosponsor, and recommend volunteering to a friend or colleague.

We note, however, that men are also slightly more likely to rate the experience as a poor one at the other end of the scale. We suggest that the gender differences could be attributed to more than one factor. Women could have had a better experience overall, or individual respondents could have had more varied experiences (some great, some poor), or respondents could simply have less ambivalence about their experiences, either good or poor. In all comparisons, the standard deviation for responses is greater for women than for men, particularly for the question about recommending volunteering to a colleague.

The differences could also be due to the ways that women are socialized to respond to experiences (including survey responses). It would be premature to conclude that women are more easily satisfied with their volunteer experience than men until you examine your methods of volunteer recognition and support within your own organization. If you find them both adequate and equitable, your conclusions might be different.

EXHIBIT 6.18

How satisfied are you with the following aspects of your volunteer experience with [cosponsor]?

Asked only of those who reported either current or past volunteer activity with the cosponsor. Mean shows the average rating on a 1–5 scale with 5=very satisfied.

	Male		Female	
	Mean	Rank	Mean	Rank
Helping you to feel that you are giving back to your profession	3.78	1	3.95	1
Having opportunities to meet, work, and socialize with others in your field or profession	3.77	2	3.92	2
Working with others toward a common goal	3.68	3	3.92	3
Using your existing skills	3.65	4	3.86	4
Feeling respected, appreciated, and valued	3.48	6	3.73	5
Ability to make choices about when you volunteer	3.42	8	3.70	6
Opportunity to take a leadership role	3.50	5	3.68	7
Helping you to connect with the mission of the organization	3.42	7	3.65	8
Ability to make choices about what you do as a volunteer	3.41	9	3.63	9
Learning new skills	3.35	10	3.59	10
Receiving training needed to be effective	3.06	12	3.35	11
Receiving feedback about your performance	3.10	11	3.33	12
Receiving incentives like stipends, transportation, and/or meals	2.73	13	2.95	13

EXHIBIT 6.19

Please use the scale provided below to rate your overall satisfaction with volunteering for [cosponsor].

	Male	Female
	%	%
Very dissatisfied	1.8	1.5
2	7.2	5.7
3	37.1	35.5
4	38.2	34.2
Very satisfied	15.8	23.2

EXHIBIT 6.21

How likely is it that you would recommend volunteering for [cosponsor] to a friend or colleague?

	Male	Female
	%	%
Very unlikely	19.1	19.9
2	18.8	17.4
3	30.9	30.8
4	18.4	16.6
Very likely	12.8	15.4

EXHIBIT 6.20

How likely is it that you will be a volunteer for [cosponsor] within the next 12 months?

	Male	Female
	%	%
Very unlikely	27.6	28.3
2	22.1	20.1
3	25.3	25.3
4	11.8	12.5
Very likely	13.2	13.7

Three Parting Thoughts

We make three conclusions from this analysis about the relationship between gender, family status, and volunteering behavior. First, this chapter demonstrates the value in comparing general volunteering behavior to association volunteering. The slight and subtle differences found between men and women when we examined community volunteering were magnified in the context of association volunteering—particularly with respect to the extent of their service.

Second, on the question of gender, women in our sample behave similarly to other national studies in responding more positively about volunteerism. Men behave similarly to other national studies by volunteering more hours than women and for more organizations—with this difference particularly pronounced for association volunteering. As expected, men and women are recruited into volunteering in slightly different ways, and they have different preferences about the kind of volunteer work they perform. However, they do agree about which motivations for volunteering are most important. We find a substantial gender difference for non-volunteers, where men are more likely than women never to have volunteered.

As we have already remarked, we cannot tell to what extent this gender difference is due to the ways in which men and women are socialized to civic activity. In some respects, this will not matter to you: If men and women in your member ranks have different preferred volunteer tasks, your job is to ensure that they have those options. On the other hand, it will be important for you to understand when the differences in volunteer behavior and satisfaction are due to societal expectations, parental status or upbringing, or, conversely, when they are due to present opportunities or lack of opportunity. Members who feel excluded from volunteer opportunities due to any factor—their marital or parental status, gender, or age—are more likely to depart unhappy. Organizations that already pay attention to principles of equity and diversity within their member ranks may find that they are further ahead in understanding how to involve members as volunteers most effectively. If not, it may be helpful to look first at whether the minority gender in your organization—whether men or women—feels included (this study includes 23 quite different organizations with respect to gender distribution).

Third and finally, on the question of marital and family status, we expected to find a crowding-out effect with respect to the impact of family responsibilities on volunteering connected to professional work. Although we did find a small effect, more than two thirds of the respondents who are actively raising children expressed interest in connecting volunteering to their professional work. The message from this encouraging result is not to write off the busy parent. Although association members with children could be more difficult to recruit into professionally oriented volunteer activities, many parents—particularly those who have temporarily left the workforce to raise children—look to volunteering as a means of staying connected to their profession. We also note that the number of hours of service performed by respondents varied very little according to marital status, family volunteering, or children. Organizations wishing to capture the time and talent of parents as volunteers must be adept at offering enough flexibility of choice and organizational support to meet their needs. We suggest, for instance, that you not assume that the new parent is uninterested in volunteering, since you risk losing this individual later on when he or she regains some free time. It might be more strategic to maintain a relationship with the too-busy people and contact them later.

ACTING ON THE FINDINGS
Gender and Family Composition

To develop a volunteer strategy responsive to family situation, associations might consider asking members to prioritize their preferences. When combined with demographic data about your members, these preferences can then be analyzed to understand patterns in your organization. Care should be taken to avoid assumptions about the kinds of activities that members will prefer, particularly with respect to gender.

Think about the time commitments of volunteer tasks and how they can be designed to be family-friendly. (The tool included here is one aid you might use.) Some suggestions and questions:

- Do your bylaws require members to be present at committee and board meetings? Could bylaws be revised to permit attendance via telecommunications devices?

- At what time of day are your meetings held? How might your logistical decisions affect the participation of certain members?

- Conduct a communication audit on your volunteer marketing materials. Are there any gender or family-cycle biases apparent?

- Are men and women participating in association activities in equal proportion to their membership representation? In other words, are there hidden biases in the way that men or women are recruited into volunteer tasks?

- When decisions are made or activities planned that might have a particularly strong impact on certain demographic groups, are these groups represented in the decision-making process?

To provide flexible options ideal for volunteers with family obligations, your organization might consider the identification and/or creation of volunteer opportunities custom-tailored to this high-potential group. Use the following planning sheet to match volunteer opportunities to volunteers based on their probable time commitment.

Planning Flexible Volunteer Options

Time Requirement	Virtual Volunteer Activities	Face-to-Face Volunteer Activities
1–12 hours	1) *ex.* Edit articles 2) 3) 4) 5)	1) *ex.* Work at local education program 2) 3) 4) 5)
13–49 hours	1) *ex.* Serve as a virtual mentor 2) 3) 4) 5)	1) 2) 3) 4) 5)
50–99 hours	1) 2) 3) 4) 5)	1) *ex.* Plan a local symposium 2) 3) 4) 5)
100–249 hours	1) 2) 3) 4) 5)	1) 2) 3) 4) 5)
250–499 hours	1) 2) 3) 4) 5)	1) 2) 3) 4) 5)
500+ hours	1) *ex.* Write a book 2) 3) 4) 5)	1) *ex.* Serve as local chapter officer 2) 3) 4) 5)

CHAPTER 7

Employer Type

ASSOCIATION MEMBERS WORK IN quite varied professional settings. How does the difference influence their volunteer activity? We approached the question from two perspectives. First, researchers have speculated that some economic sectors—particularly the public and nonprofit sectors—attract individuals with more pro-social values (Rotolo and Wilson 2006). Not only might these individuals volunteer more, but the organizations they work for might also actively support their employees' volunteer behavior through their managerial practices or by connecting volunteerism explicitly to their mission. If sector matters, the industry employing an association member can influence the amount of general or professional volunteer activity a member pursues. This would be a useful connection to find in this study to help you understand which of your members might be most likely to volunteer for association activities.

We might also look at how an association member's employment sector and occupation influences the activities in which he or she is interested. Since part of your challenge in engaging members in volunteer activities is to understand which tasks they prefer and accomplish proficiently, it would be useful to understand the connection between a member's industry and interests as you design your volunteer recruitment strategies.

From either perspective, keep in mind that volunteerism is, in large part, a function of personal characteristics that are linked to socio-economic status but not necessarily linked to employment status. It is difficult to make a causal connection between employer type and volunteer activity unless we have controlled for all of the competing explanations—and, as this study has already concluded, there are many (including family responsibilities, upbringing, work hours, geographic distance to volunteer opportunities, etc.). Volunteerism is also dependent on some factors that we have not captured in this study, particularly the more specific degrees of difference from employer to employer in how an employee's volunteerism is supported.

In THE DECISION TO VOLUNTEER study, we asked respondents several questions about their employment status: at what career level they were (from entry-level to senior-level), how long they had been in their profession, and in what kind of organization they were employed: private industry, academic or educational, nonprofit, government, or self-employed. It is principally this latter question that we explore in this chapter.[1] We did not capture specific information about their occupation (e.g., teacher, manager, nurse, trainer, etc.). On a further important methodological note, the analysis presented in this chapter excludes those respondents who are unemployed, retired, or students (4.4 percent of all respondents).

Although this is a more limited analysis than we have performed in some other chapters, this chapter produces some useful information about how employment field influences the choices of volunteer tasks that association members make, and the means by which they can be recruited as volunteers. At the end of this chapter, we offer some suggestions about how employers can support professional volunteering through incentives and policies.

Demographic Profile of Members by Employment Sector

Approximately half (49.7 percent) of the employed respondents are in the private sector (see Chapter 3, Exhibit 3.9). Of the remainder, 19.5 percent are in educational organizations, 13 percent self-employed or in

solo practice, 10.8 percent in nonprofit organizations, and 7 percent in government.

As shown in Exhibit 7.1, the educational levels of respondents vary considerably according to employment sector, with the greatest number of terminal degrees (such as doctorates) in the academic/educational field or in solo practice. We also see a considerable variation across employment sector in the gender distribution of our respondents, ranging from nearly 72 percent men among those who are in solo practice or the private sector, to nearly 72 percent women in the nonprofit sector (Exhibit 7.2).[2] Those respondents in education, solo practice, and nonprofits are slightly older than the average in our sample (Exhibit 7.3). Nonprofits and those in solo practice also constitute the oldest employment groups in terms of the number of years in which they have been working in their profession

EXHIBIT 7.1

Which of the following best describes your highest level of education?

	Private sector/ private industry	Academia/ educational institution/ school*	Nonprofit organization	Government	Self-employed, solo practice, or independent consultant
	%	%	%	%	%
High school or less	2.0	8.6	0.8	1.3	1.4
Some college	6.0	11.0	2.5	4.3	4.5
Associate degree or equivalent	7.9	6.6	15.5	4.1	6.2
Bachelor's degree or equivalent	42.5	13.9	31.7	35.6	24.1
Master's degree or equivalent	31.5	30.3	41.8	44.2	19.6
PhD, JD, EdD, or equivalent	4.2	20.1	4.2	7.3	4.7
MD or DDS	5.9	9.5	3.6	3.2	39.4

*The respondents in this category include school nutritionists (32 percent), school principals (17 percent), college professors and researchers, physicians (9 percent), nurses, school teachers, and other groups.

---

[1] With this question, we note that there could be more than one correct category (a respondent could be employed in a public school and could mark either "educational" or "government"). Our survey participants were asked to pick the response that best describes their workplace.

---

[2] Across the U.S., using 1989 data, 67 percent of nonprofit employees and 43 percent of for-profit employees were female (Leete 2006).

EXHIBIT 7.2

Gender by Employment Sector

	Private sector/ private industry	Academia/ educational institution/ school	Nonprofit organization	Government	Self-employed, solo practice, or independent consultant
	%	%	%	%	%
Male	71.1	36.5	28.3	59.9	71.6
Female	28.9	63.5	71.7	40.1	28.4

EXHIBIT 7.3

Age by Employment Sector

	Private sector/ private industry	Academia/ educational institution/ school	Nonprofit organization	Government	Self-employed, solo practice, or independent consultant
	%	%	%	%	%
Pre-war (1945 or before)	4.5	8.1	5.7	3.8	14.1
Early Boom (1946–1954)	21.3	32.8	31.9	22.8	27.1
Late Boom (1955–1962)	29.6	29.4	33.0	31.0	31.0
Gen X (1963–1976)	35.7	25.5	24.8	35.3	25.6
Millennials (1977 or later)	8.9	4.1	4.6	7.0	2.3

(Exhibit 7.4). Other employment characteristics such as career level and employment status show little difference across employment fields, with the exception of those in solo practice, who are more likely to be employed part time (not shown).

Volunteering Across Employment Sectors

Our respondents vary only slightly across employment fields and sectors in terms of whether they are actively volunteering (Exhibit 7.5). Across employment fields and sectors, we see little difference in the tasks that volunteers perform (results not shown), but we do see some difference in the extent of their volunteer activity. As shown in Exhibit 7.6, those in solo practice, educational, and nonprofit organizations volunteer for more organizations than those in private practice or government.

EXHIBIT 7.4

In what year did you begin working in the profession or industry in which you are now employed?

	Private sector/ private industry	Academia/ educational institution/ school	Nonprofit organization	Government	Self-employed, solo practice, or independent consultant
	%	%	%	%	%
Before 1980	20.7	24.2	30.9	18.6	28.0
1980–1989	29.8	26.0	28.2	30.8	32.9
1990–1999	28.5	27.7	24.5	28.8	22.4
2000 or later	21.1	22.2	16.4	21.8	16.8

EXHIBIT 7.5

Have you volunteered for any organization?

	Private sector/ private industry	Academia/ educational institution/ school	Nonprofit organization	Government	Self-employed, solo practice, or independent consultant
	%	%	%	%	%
In the last 12 months	73.2	82.1	80.1	76.7	79.5
In the past but not in the last 12 months	17.1	12.1	13.2	15.7	14.4
Never volunteered	9.8	5.8	6.7	7.7	6.1

Some of the differences across employment fields could also be associated with age and gender differences. For example, the educational and nonprofit fields have more female employees. One could also assume an association between volunteering and self-employment. Exhibit 7.6 reminds us that the financial pressures of self-employment do not necessarily preclude active volunteerism. As we see here, those in solo practice are particularly active volunteers when compared to other fields of employment. This relationship can also be due to the number of medical personnel in this category who have found ways to connect their professional work to volunteerism. However, we also find from Exhibit 7.7 that while those in educational and nonprofit organizations (the other employment fields in which volunteers are most active) are more likely to report that volunteering has had a positive impact on their careers, the same does not hold true for the self-employed. Their responses to this question about volunteer benefits are positive, but they agree less strongly than do those in education and nonprofits about whether volunteering supports their career. The

EXHIBIT 7.6

For how many different organizations did you perform volunteer work in the last 12 months?

	Private sector/ private industry	Academia/ educational institution/ school	Nonprofit organization	Government	Self-employed, solo practice, or independent consultant
	%	%	%	%	%
One	21.8	13.6	17.9	20.8	16.5
Two	32.7	32.4	29.8	33.1	26.4
Three	26.7	30.8	29.9	27.0	29.1
Four	11.3	13.2	13.1	12.7	13.4
Five or more	7.5	9.9	9.3	6.4	14.6

EXHIBIT 7.7

What effect do you think volunteering has had on your career or, if you are self-employed, on your business?

	Private sector/ private industry	Academia/ educational institution/ school	Nonprofit organization	Government	Self-employed, solo practice, or independent consultant
	%	%	%	%	%
Very negative	0.1	0.1	0.0	0.1	0.3
2	0.9	0.9	0.8	1.3	0.9
3	18.1	10.8	10.3	16.4	15.4
4	32.6	25.0	26.6	29.3	30.7
Very Positive	48.3	63.1	62.4	52.9	52.6

responses of those in the private sector are similar—positive, but lower than other employment environments, perhaps evidence that volunteering competes with their career or is not supported by their employer.

Volunteering for the Cosponsor

We see a more striking difference across employment fields when we compare activities and hours for cosponsor volunteering. First, those in education are more likely to have volunteered for a cosponsor organization now or in the past (Exhibit 7.8). A total of 57.4 percent of those in educational fields have volunteered for a cosponsor organization, compared to 40–47 percent employed in other environments. There was very little difference across employer types with respect to the method of recruitment by which respondents entered cosponsor volunteering, with the exception that those in education were more likely to have been asked to volunteer by association staff members, and those in solo practice were more likely to have been recruited by other volunteers (results not shown). This personal method of recruitment is generally considered to be effective but underused.

EXHIBIT 7.8

Any Volunteering for Cosponsor—Now or in the Past

	Private sector/ private industry	Academia/ educational institution/ school	Nonprofit organization	Government	Self-employed, solo practice, or independent consultant
	%	%	%	%	%
No	59.3	42.6	56.6	53.4	57.1
Yes	40.7	57.4	43.4	46.6	42.9

In Exhibit 7.9, we have compared employment fields according to the volunteer activities members perform for a cosponsor organization. Those in education are more likely than others to report volunteering for the cosponsor. These respondents report involvement in every single association activity with greater frequency than any other employment

EXHIBIT 7.9

In the last 12 months, have you done any of the following as a volunteer (in person, online, or in any other way) on behalf of [cosponsor]?

Respondent checked all that apply.

	Private sector/ private industry		Academia/ educational institution/ school		Nonprofit organization		Government		Self-employed, solo practice, or independent consultant	
	%	Rank	%	Rank	%	Rank	%	Rank	%	Rank
Provided mentoring, coaching, or tutoring for members, students, or others	10.8	1	20.7	1	15.2	2	14.7	1	13.4	2
Recruited a member or members	10.5	2	20.7	2	16.1	1	12.7	2	7.8	4
Provided professional advice	10.0	3	19.7	3	12.8	3	12.2	3	13.8	1
Served on a committee for a local chapter or section	9.0	4	19.5	4	9.9	4	10.4	4	9.5	3
Spoke or presented a paper	7.0	5	15.3	5	7.1	7	9.2	5	7.6	5
Participated in a discussion group, expert panel, or report	7.0	6	15.2	6	7.8	5	8.3	6	7.3	6
Reviewed a paper or proposal for a publication	4.2	11	13.1	7	3.7	11	4.6	10	3.8	12
Raised funds	4.3	10	12.4	8	7.4	6	3.9	12	4.2	11
Served on the board for a local chapter or section	6.5	7	12.3	9	6.1	8	6.3	7	6.7	7
Submitted a paper or manuscript for publication	3.2	14	12.0	10	2.8	15	3.8	13	4.4	10
Moderated or facilitated discussion groups at meetings or elsewhere	5.1	8	11.3	11	5.6	9	6.1	8	6.1	8
Reviewed research, conducted literature review, or resource reviews, or analyzed data	2.9	15	9.4	12	3.1	14	3.3	15	3.0	15
Reviewed proposals for conferences or projects	3.7	12	8.9	13	3.3	12	4.5	11	3.2	14
Served on a committee for the parent organization	3.5	13	8.5	14	4.0	10	3.7	14	4.5	9
Reviewed applications as part of accreditation, certification, or competitive program	2.1	16	7.1	15	2.2	16	2.7	16	2.1	16
Wrote proposals, grant applications, or business plans	1.7	17	7.0	16	2.2	17	2.3	17	1.9	19
Served on a technical committee or reviewed standards and practices	4.4	9	6.9	17	3.2	13	5.2	9	3.3	13
Made a presentation or testified on behalf of the organization to any legislative body (local, state, national, or global advocacy)	1.4	18	4.8	18	1.8	18	2.2	18	2.0	17
Served on the board for the parent organization	1.1	20	2.6	19	1.3	19	1.6	20	2.0	18
Prepared background for regulators, the press, or others	1.2	19	2.2	20	1.1	20	1.9	19	1.6	20

environment. The results suggest that those employed in educational institutions—teachers, administrators, nutritionists, and professors from secondary to higher education—constitute a particularly important source of association volunteers across a range of activities. This connection is likely to hold true in your association to the extent that your mission is related to research, training, teaching, credentialing, and similar educational activities.

Despite their greater range of activity, those employed in educational institutions are not providing the majority of volunteer hours: as Exhibit 7.10 demonstrates, the volunteer hours performed for cosponsors are quite evenly distributed across employment fields with the exception of nonprofit employees, who appear to provide slightly fewer hours at the high end of the scale. Rather, respondents employed in educational institutions are engaged in a wider selection of association activities. We see one of the possible reasons for their greater involvement when we compare responses to the survey question about virtual or electronic volunteering (Exhibit 7.11). Those in educational institutions are the most likely to have taken advantage of the Internet and other electronic tools to volunteer (nearly 24 percent, compared to 16–20 percent in other employment environments).

EXHIBIT 7.10

On average, how many hours did you perform volunteer work for [cosponsor] in the last 12 months?

	Private sector/ private industry	Academia/ educational institution/ school	Nonprofit organization	Government	Self-employed, solo practice, or independent consultant
	%	%	%	%	%
1–12 hours	56.7	54.2	64.0	60.4	59.8
13–49 hours	27.0	28.6	22.3	24.8	23.5
50–99 hours	9.6	11.1	9.9	9.4	10.0
100–249 hours	4.9	4.4	2.9	4.0	4.8
250 or more hours	1.8	1.6	.8	1.3	2.0

EXHIBIT 7.11

Have you performed any volunteer work for [cosponsor] by "virtual volunteering," e.g. volunteer activities that are completed, in whole or in part, via the Internet on a home, work, or public access computer?

	Private sector/ private industry	Academia/ educational institution/ school	Nonprofit organization	Government	Self-employed, solo practice, or independent consultant
	%	%	%	%	%
Yes	17.2	23.6	17.7	19.5	16.5
No	82.8	76.4	82.3	80.5	83.5

Employment Sector and the Motivation to Volunteer

Given the various explanations we have offered regarding the way individuals are motivated to volunteer, we make very tentative suggestions about the influence of employment field on the perceived benefits of volunteering. The arguments for some differences across the sectors rest in the strong likelihood that people are drawn to different occupations because of differences in their attraction to mission-oriented work. This relationship has been observed in other research and has been useful in explaining the sorting behavior we see within many occupational fields and across the business, public, and nonprofit sectors. In a nutshell, if certain kinds of people are drawn to certain professions, these differences may also influence their attraction to civic service.

Exhibit 7.12 displays a comparison across employment fields of the responses to questions we posed through the Volunteer Functions Inventory. As we have previously, we compare the potential benefits across six dimensions and also compare members' responses to the perceived benefits of community volunteering and the benefits of volunteering for a cosponsor association. Keep in mind that we have already observed that gender has a strong influence on volunteer motivations and our employment environments vary considerably in terms of the gender distribution.

When we compare employment environments, we find two results that are similar to our other analyses in this volume. Across sectors and fields

EXHIBIT 7.12

Volunteer Functions Inventory (VFI)*

Regardless of your previous volunteer experience, how important or accurate would the following statements be for you in doing volunteer work?

By Employment Sector (Excludes Retired, Students, and Unemployed)

VFI Dimensions		Private Sector		Academia/Education		Nonprofit		Government		Self Employed	
		Volunteering in general	Volunteering for cosponsor	Volunteering in general	Volunteering for cosponsor	Volunteering in general	Volunteering for cosponsor	Volunteering in general	Volunteering for cosponsor	Volunteering in general	Volunteering for cosponsor
		Mean	Mean	Mean	Mean	Mean	Mean	Mean	Mean	Mean	Mean
Values	I feel it is important to help others	4.32	3.75	4.44	4.02	4.48	4.10	4.36	3.97	4.43	3.88
	I can do something for a profession or cause that is important to me	4.02	3.83	4.21	4.06	4.25	4.07	4.08	3.97	4.20	3.93
	I feel compassion toward people in need	3.98	3.34	4.19	3.73	4.32	3.83	4.01	3.52	4.12	3.49
Understanding	Volunteering allows me to gain a new perspective on things	3.82	3.34	3.94	3.52	4.02	3.60	3.93	3.52	3.82	3.24
	I can explore my own strengths	3.39	3.18	3.50	3.35	3.61	3.45	3.54	3.37	3.12	2.98
	I can learn new skills through direct, hands-on experience	3.34	3.25	3.48	3.35	3.49	3.36	3.48	3.39	3.09	2.90
Enhancement	Volunteering makes me feel needed	3.08	2.67	3.34	2.89	3.36	2.87	3.20	2.78	3.05	2.55
	Volunteering brings me satisfaction or recognition that I do not get at work	3.12	2.68	3.13	2.74	3.24	2.83	3.25	2.82	2.95	2.41
Career	I can make new contacts that might help my business or career	2.73	3.04	2.73	2.84	2.71	2.94	2.63	2.92	2.72	2.68
	Volunteer experience looks good on my resume	2.34	2.51	2.56	2.64	2.64	2.65	2.49	2.70	1.97	2.07
	Volunteering helps me to explore different career options	2.28	2.44	2.35	2.44	2.33	2.56	2.39	2.66	1.78	1.83
	Volunteering gives a competitive advantage to my business	2.25	2.55	2.17	2.40	2.21	2.39	2.08	2.35	2.16	2.25
	Volunteering can help me get my foot in the door at a place where I would like to work	2.04	2.30	2.15	2.30	2.06	2.28	2.15	2.44	1.66	1.82
Social	Volunteering is important to the people I respect	3.20	3.00	3.46	3.23	3.43	3.27	3.29	3.09	3.26	3.02
Protective	Volunteering helps me deal with some of my own problems	2.33	2.12	2.38	2.22	2.26	2.08	2.38	2.12	2.06	1.84

*The VFI compares volunteers according to what they believe they gain through volunteer work. Mean shows the average rating on a 1–5 scale with 5=very important. The 15 questions were rated by respondents twice in the survey. First, all respondents were asked about "volunteering in general." Later in the survey, the same questions were asked of respondents who currently volunteer for the cosponsor OR who have volunteered for the cosponsor anytime in the past. Items are grouped according to the six underlying dimensions identified in the Volunteer Functions Inventory (see Bibliography: Clary, Snyder, and Stukas 1996).

of employment, respondents are less likely to find cosponsor volunteering valuable when compared to community volunteering. And the order in which members rank the benefits of volunteering has not changed, with the Values and Understanding dimensions ranked most highly.

We do find some differences across sectors and fields of employment in terms of the relative value that respondents assign to these volunteer motivations. A preliminary analysis finds that employment sector matters even after controlling for these factors. Private sector employees, both employed and self-employed, assign lower value to questions on the Values and Understanding dimensions, and they assign and higher values to questions on the Career dimension. The results suggest that those in the private sector appear to be more strongly attracted to career- and business-related reasons for volunteering. Although Exhibit 7.12 suggests that educational, nonprofit, and government employees assign higher values to questions on the Values and Understanding dimensions, the difference does not hold after controlling for personal characteristics.[3] In other words, private sector employees appear to behave differently, but the jury is still out on those in educational, nonprofit, and government settings.

Satisfaction with Volunteering Across Employment Fields

This section addresses the relationship between employment field and a respondent's satisfaction with volunteering. As we have observed, it would be premature to make a causal connection between an employment field and a predisposition toward volunteering without accounting for the influence of a number of additional supportive factors (especially those dependent on the employer). Nonetheless, professionals working in associations will find it useful to understand whether the greater level of volunteering activity within some employment fields (particularly the educational field) translates to a higher level of satisfaction with volunteering. The alternative—a lower level of satisfaction—might indicate some burnout within active volunteer groups.

The results do not suggest burnout. Employees in education, followed by nonprofit employees, are slightly more likely to be satisfied with their cosponsor volunteering experience than those in other fields (Exhibit 7.13). They are substantially more likely to say that they intend to continue volunteering for a cosponsor when compared to employees from other fields (Exhibit 7.14). They are also more likely to indicate that they would recommend cosponsor volunteering to a friend or colleague (Exhibit 7.15). And they are most likely, in comparison to other groups, to indicate satisfaction with specific aspects of their volunteer experience (Exhibit 7.16). These

EXHIBIT 7.13

Please use the scale provided below to rate your overall satisfaction with volunteering for [cosponsor].

	Private sector/ private industry	Academia/ educational institution/ school	Nonprofit organization	Government	Self-employed, solo practice, or independent consultant
	%	%	%	%	%
Very dissatisfied	1.7	1.3	1.2	2.7	2.8
2	7.1	4.7	5.3	6.9	9.6
3	38.5	33.4	35.3	33.6	35.4
4	36.8	37.0	36.8	37.2	35.5
Very satisfied	15.8	23.6	21.2	19.7	16.7

---

[3] The analysis was performed on selected VFI questions using OLS regression. Only VFI questions related to cosponsor volunteering (Survey question 18) were analyzed. We controlled for age, gender, family volunteering, education, community volunteering, and volunteer hours.

EXHIBIT 7.14

How likely is it that you will be a volunteer for [cosponsor] within the next 12 months?

	Private sector/ private industry	Academia/ educational institution/ school	Nonprofit organization	Government	Self-employed, solo practice, or independent consultant
	%	%	%	%	%
Very unlikely	27.7	21.4	22.8	26.2	33.0
2	22.4	17.8	22.0	20.8	22.8
3	26.3	24.8	29.0	26.0	23.6
4	11.5	15.8	13.8	11.9	9.2
Very likely	12.0	20.2	12.4	15.2	11.4

EXHIBIT 7.15

How likely is it that you would recommend volunteering for [cosponsor] to a friend or colleague?

	Private sector/ private industry	Academia/ educational institution/ school	Nonprofit organization	Government	Self-employed, solo practice, or independent consultant
	%	%	%	%	%
Very unlikely	19.3	15.6	16.2	18.1	23.2
2	19.9	15.2	16.5	17.4	19.6
3	31.8	29.7	34.3	28.3	29.7
4	17.3	20.5	18.4	19.7	14.3
Very likely	11.7	19.1	14.6	16.6	13.3

EXHIBIT 7.16

How satisfied are you with the following aspects of your volunteer experience with [cosponsor]?

Asked only of those who either reported performing one or more of the listed cosponsor volunteer activities in the last 12 months OR who reported volunteering for the cosponsor at some time in the past.
Mean shows the average rating on a 1–5 scale with 5=very satisfied.

	Private sector/ private industry		Academia/ educational institution/school		Nonprofit organization		Government		Self-employed, solo practice, or independent consultant	
	Mean	Rank	Mean	Rank	Mean	Rank	Mean	Rank	Mean	Rank
Helping you to feel that you are giving back to your profession	3.77	2	3.94	1	3.94	1	3.84	2	3.85	1
Having opportunities to meet, work, and socialize with others in your field or profession	3.80	1	3.92	2	3.85	4	3.86	1	3.79	2
Working with others toward a common goal	3.71	3	3.89	3	3.89	2	3.77	3	3.70	3
Using your existing skills	3.66	4	3.85	4	3.86	3	3.72	4	3.65	4
Feeling respected, appreciated, and valued	3.52	6	3.69	5	3.70	5	3.60	5	3.47	5
Helping you to connect with the mission of the organization	3.41	9	3.66	6	3.70	6	3.52	9	3.42	8
Opportunity to take a leadership role	3.54	5	3.65	7	3.68	8	3.56	8	3.44	6
Ability to make choices about when you volunteer	3.49	7	3.61	8	3.69	7	3.56	7	3.43	7
Ability to make choices about what you do as a volunteer	3.47	8	3.57	9	3.61	9	3.57	6	3.38	9
Learning new skills	3.39	10	3.57	10	3.56	10	3.50	10	3.26	10
Receiving training needed to be effective	3.09	12	3.36	11	3.34	11	3.23	12	3.02	12
Receiving feedback about your performance	3.14	11	3.30	12	3.33	12	3.27	11	3.09	11
Receiving incentives like stipends, transportation, and/or meals	2.78	13	2.97	13	2.91	13	2.82	13	2.62	13

results also support the argument we first introduced in Chapter 4 that the more actively involved volunteers are generally the most satisfied.

By contrast, those respondents from the private sector, whether employed or self-employed, are the least likely to say that they are satisfied with aspects of their volunteer experience. We do not see substantial differences here, but we do see a consistent pattern across employment fields wherein those in private sector and solo practice are less likely to report satisfaction with volunteering (such as receiving feedback or training, learning new skills, or having opportunities to take a leadership role or to develop a social/professional network through volunteering). This connection between field of employment and satisfaction with the volunteering experience holds true even after controlling for other demographic or occupational factors, particularly in the two fields of education and self-employment.[4]

Does Employment Field Predict Volunteerism?

We introduced earlier the idea that some employment fields might support greater volunteering behavior. In Exhibit 7.17, we compare the likelihood of volunteering for any organization, volunteering for the cosponsor, and anticipated future volunteering for the cosponsor according to employment field. Even after controlling for various other explanatory factors such as family volunteering and gender, the field of employment matters. Those in educational fields are more likely to volunteer for their member association (Column 2) and to intend to continue volunteering (Column 3). Those who are self-employed or in solo practice are less likely to volunteer for their professional association or to intend to continue to volunteer. Those in the private sector or employed by nonprofits are also less likely to volunteer for a cosponsor when compared to other employment fields but potentially just as likely to volunteer in the future.

---

[4] Based on a regression analysis on various volunteer satisfaction questions. Controlling for age, gender, family volunteering, children, educational status, community volunteering, years in profession, and hours of volunteer activity performed for the cosponsor, those in academic fields were more satisfied and those who are self-employed are less satisfied with cosponsor volunteering.

EXHIBIT 7.17

Predicting Volunteering as a Function of Employment Sector

	(1) Volunteering for any organization	(2) Volunteering for cosponsor	(3) Future intention of volunteering for cosponsor
Employment Sector			
Private sector		−	
Academic/educational		+	+
Nonprofit		−	
Government			
Self employed		−	−
Years in profession		+	−
Socio-economic Factors			
Female	+		
Increasing age	+	+	−
Family volunteers	+	+	
Presence of children in household		−	−
Greater education	+	+	+
Volunteer Experience			
Any volunteering	N/i	+	
Number of hours volunteered	N/i	N/i	+
Satisfaction with benefits of volunteering	N/i	N/i	+

Note: Results were produced via logistic regression analysis. A "+" indicates that respondents with the characteristic are more likely to agree with the question, holding other factors constant. A "−" indicates that respondents with the characteristic are less likely to agree with that question. N/i = not included. These variables are only applicable in the third column.

Note that employment field becomes a statistically significant factor only when we look at cosponsor (professional) volunteering (Column 2) but not for community volunteering (Column 1). We would assume that this stronger connection to professional volunteering is due to potentially greater opportunities for those in any field to make a substantial contribution to their professional field as volunteers. It is more difficult to use employment field to predict general volunteering because this level of volunteering has less to do with the kinds of volunteer activities that individuals engage in outside of their professions. But this kind of outcome also makes sense when we examine, across Columns 1, 2, and 3, the diminishing impact of personal demographic factors and the growing influence of the professional arena on volunteering. In Column 1, volunteering is driven by the socio-economic characteristics discussed in Chapter 2. In Column 2, we still see the influence of these demographic characteristics on professional volunteering behavior, but we also see the influence of a member's professional environment. And in Column 3, as we would expect, education is still important because it is related to professional volunteer opportunities, but the volunteer experience itself becomes the most relevant factor in predicting future association volunteering.

What the Results Suggest

At the beginning of this chapter, we suggested several possible connections between members' field of employment and their volunteering activity. We introduced the idea that some sectors might foster more pro-social employees, and the institutions within certain sectors might also support professional volunteering more actively. We also suggested that employment field might cause some sorting behavior in terms of what activities volunteers prefer to take on. But we also argued that any causal connections between volunteer frequency and employment field are likely to be masked by other intervening factors. And we acknowledge that this survey does not capture all of the relevant information such as specific respondent occupations and details of an employer's policies toward workplace volunteering.

> *"I perceive participation in [cosponsor] activities to be very advantageous to career progression within my company."*
> **– Association member**

Our results suggest the following:

- The field or sector of employment of an association member matters in terms of who volunteers but only for professional volunteering rather than general community volunteering. Those in academic/educational fields are substantially *more* likely, and those who are self-employed are *less* likely to volunteer for a professional association (but the self-employed may volunteer more elsewhere).

- Employment field also matters in terms of how much professional service a member takes on, with those from educational fields taking on the greatest range of volunteer activities and those from the private sector and solo practice taking on the greatest number of hours (perhaps because those in solo practice are more likely to work part time). One reason for the influence of employment sector on volunteer activities may be that those in educational fields have more choice of activities that rely on their expertise and interests (e.g., research, training, credentialing). And it may also be easier for them to take advantage of virtual volunteering opportunities to the extent that their work depends on electronic communication.

- Those from the educational field are most likely to volunteer for a cosponsor, but they are also most likely to have been asked to volunteer. Opportunity alone may not get you to the finish line—you must still employ appropriate and active recruiting tools.

We assume that some, if not all, of the association volunteering that our respondents perform is conducted during work hours and may also be considered to be part of a member's professional responsibilities. To the extent this is true in your association, the degree to which employers support workplace volunteering will matter. Corporate volunteer programs have increased in scope and quality substantially during the past decade. Businesses employ a wide variety of policies and tactics to encourage employees to volunteer, ranging from tacit permission all the way up to paid time off, formal pro bono programs, or fully fledged, professionally staffed corporate volunteer programs.

When workplace volunteering might once have been considered a distraction from other work responsibilities, the benefits are now more widely recognized. Although the research is still spotty, workplace volunteering is at least perceived to increase morale and reduce turnover among employees, to improve community visibility and credibility of the employer, and to improve the communities in which employees reside (Tschirhart 2005). The impact on associations is not well understood since little research has attempted to link workplace volunteering to professional volunteering activity (as opposed to more general community volunteering). In one recent survey of Fortune 500 companies, the consulting firm Deloitte (2008) found that employers were very receptive to workplace volunteering when it could support talent development within their ranks. However, only one in six employers offered the kinds of skills-based volunteering opportunities to staff that could support professional development. We suggest that association volunteering can help make the connection. Have you contacted any HR staff recently?

Employees report that the most important factor an employer can offer to encourage workplace volunteering—including, presumably, association volunteering—is material support from employers, including release time.

> **"My employer does not give time off for volunteering. It has to be done on our own time."**
>
> **– Survey respondent**

Employers can increase workplace volunteering by developing strategies and policies that communicate the value of volunteering to employees and that help employees fulfill their volunteer commitments. Strategies for involving employees should change to meet their various motivations and expectations. For example, newly hired employees might be particularly interested in team-based volunteer projects because they allow for social interaction, but the employer might be equally interested in an opportunity to socialize this new employee into its business culture. Other employees might be recruited to volunteering through material rewards or status rewards such as public recognition. In addition, some employers are able to recognize the more ideological and less material motivations of employees by offering matching incentive programs that make financial donations to causes in which employees volunteer a certain number of hours (Peterson 2004). Whatever the strategy, the key is to understand how to materially connect an employee's work responsibilities to volunteer efforts that support his or her profession.

Employer Type

To attract members from other fields of employment besides educational institutions, you will have to learn what motivates these professionals to get engaged. You must understand how to communicate your volunteer opportunities to those in various professional fields in terms that have relevance for them. Certainly, you will have to compete with the greater time pressures of the solo practitioner. And while they represent a diverse group and generalizations are difficult, those in the public and nonprofit sectors may be particularly well prepared to recognize the mission-related benefits of volunteering because they are accustomed to connecting mission to their work in their own occupations. Those in the private sector may be more attuned to tangible benefits of volunteering—and also more likely to volunteer when their employer recognizes the benefits of volunteering.

Connecting Employment and Volunteering

Given the multitude of reasons that members express for volunteering, it is not easy to make direct connections between their volunteerism efforts and employment sector. However, in some instances in this chapter, the lessons are clearer—for instance, the idea that self-employed members are more concerned about the opportunity costs of volunteerism. Here are some suggestions for incorporating the data collected here into member outreach in the future:

- Do you have volunteer tasks that can be matched to employer type? Consider assessing your current volunteer workforce by their employer type and volunteer role. Use this information to help you target new volunteers by matching their employer type to task.

- When considering employer type, look for potential difficulties in volunteering for your organization that your members may face depending on their workplace culture. For example, if your membership includes government employees, investigate the procedures that they have to go through to be an active member of your organization. You may have to work through some legal barriers, but there may also be ways to make their involvement in your organization easier.

Interacting With Your Members' Employers

Reviewing the way your organization interacts with your members' employers is also helpful. Future outreach should account for any corporate membership programs that you may have in place and the communications you send not only to the member but to your member's place of business. Including employers in public relations and marketing activities—for example, sending an employer a press release when a member wins an association award—may increase their understanding about the professional benefits of association volunteering and increase their support for employee involvement in association activities. Consider these questions and suggestions:

- How skill-based are your volunteer opportunities? Consider asking volunteers what professional and workplace skills they would like to work on (e.g., strategic planning, meeting management, board leadership, delegation, team management).

- Do respondents' perceptions of volunteering and its effect on their career change if the volunteer activity is done during work hours versus on their own time?

- Do the typical number of hours worked weekly influence the number of hours that an individual volunteers? If there is a correlation, can you target groups based on workweek duration?

- Does your organization have a corporate membership? If so, is it time to revisit your corporate membership programs particularly with respect to volunteer recruitment strategies?

- For the self-employed and other volunteers on whom service activities have a direct financial impact, how can you make their participation as efficient and valuable to them as possible?

CHAPTER 8

The Geography of Volunteering

WITHIN THE UNITED STATES, the geographic location of a respondent may matter in many small ways with respect to volunteer activity. Association members will find varying opportunities for volunteering depending on how rural or urban a region they live in, the size of their chapters or sections, and other factors. Family and professional geographical stability might influence a member's ability to volunteer consistently for one organization. We also find some moderate differences in volunteering rates in state-by-state comparisons within the United States (Grimm et al., 2007). But, generally, volunteering within the United States tends to be less dependent on location than on the socio-economic factors we have explored in this study.

Outside the United States, volunteerism is largely shaped by societal values. Cultural norms vary from country to country with respect to civic activity, and these differences substantially influence both the frequency of volunteerism and the nature of the activities in which individuals are involved.[1] Volunteering is also a public-benefit activity that is driven in many respects by the public policies, messages, and incentives or disincentives offered by formal institutions—governments, schools, and employers. The legal status of volunteers and nongovernmental organizations varies considerably from nation to nation, and these differences will influence the

---

[1] In some countries, for example, more informal, non-institutional volunteering occurs around family members because of cultural imperatives to care for the elderly.

volunteer behavior of association members. Appealing to members outside the United States for volunteer support must take these differences into account.

Geographical differences create gaps in volunteering activity, but they also introduce opportunities. Members located in regions of the world where they do not find many professionals in their field or individuals who speak their language will seek out opportunities to connect to their peers, and volunteering offers such an opportunity. Volunteering offers a means of maintaining a professional or social network, and virtual, or online, volunteering accomplishes this for much less than the price of a plane ticket.

Cross-National Analysis

In this study of association members, our sample of non-United States citizens was shaped by the membership demographics of the sponsoring organizations. This study was not designed as a representative cross-national study of volunteers but rather as a profile of cosponsoring organizations that are largely United States-based. Depending on the international flavor of your own membership, you may find the analysis more or less applicable to your organization. Although most of the participating organizations considered themselves to be United States-based, at least one organization in our study did not. And although the United States-based associations have a large American membership base, none of them is exclusively American, and several include substantial proportions of non-United States members. As one additional caveat, we know very little about the nationality of the members who responded from outside the United States—they may be Americans living abroad, or they may hold another nationality.

Even with these limitations in mind, it is still useful to examine volunteering from a geographical perspective because geography may shape the opportunities to volunteer and thus the frequency with which members volunteer, the tasks they prefer, and how they expect associations to support their volunteer activity. Geography, in turn, should help you understand how to design volunteer programs, recruitment strategies, and recognition activities. We pose the following questions about the geography of

Geographical differences create gaps in volunteering activity, but they also introduce opportunities.

association volunteering: How does the general level of volunteering of our respondents compare across national borders? What differences do we find in the activities they choose? How might their location influence their expectations about volunteer recognition and support? And what opportunities do we find—e.g., through online volunteering—to engage members outside the United States in more association volunteering?

Demographics by Region

The members who participated in this survey are geographically representative of the full membership of the participating organizations. United States members represent 89 percent of our weighted sample, with a broad distribution across geographic regions within the United States. Outside of the United States, Canadian members are the largest group, representing one third of the non-U.S. members and 3.5 percent of the full, weighted sample. Canada has the second-largest nonprofit sector in the world and a rate of citizen volunteering similar to that of the United States (about the same number of Canadians volunteer, but they contribute more hours than Americans). Mexicans represent 0.2 percent, or a very small portion of our sample. Because the rate of volunteerism they report in this sample is similar to that of Canadian respondents, we have grouped them together for the purposes of analysis (but there are differences in these cultural groups that associations might wish to explore on their own).

Respondents from outside North America hold a diverse range of nationalities. In some countries, rates of volunteerism are similar to those in North America; in others, volunteerism is only an emerging phenomenon. Our data in this chapter will be presented in three respondent groups: United States (89.2 percent), Canada and Mexico (3.7 percent), and outside North America (7.1 percent).

Professionally, these three geographic groups are similar in some respects: About the same proportions are employed full time (88–90 percent), and career levels are similar. They differ from one another principally in their employment fields and career level. Outside the United States, respondents are more likely to work in the private sector and less likely to be employed by educational or nonprofit organizations. Outside of North America, substantially fewer respondents are self-employed (Exhibit 8.1). Those outside North America are also at slightly more senior career levels: 47.8 are at senior or CEO levels compared to 39.4 in the United States and 37.5 percent in Canada or Mexico (not shown).

EXHIBIT 8.1

Which of the following best describes the type of organization in which you are employed?

	United States	Canada and Mexico	Outside North America
	%	%	%
Private sector/private industry	47.5	61.2	71.1
Academia/educational institution/school	20.7	7.4	10.8
Nonprofit organization	11.8	3.9	2.0
Government	6.7	10.7	8.5
Self-employed, solo practice, or independent consultant	13.3	16.8	7.7

Regional demographic differences occur in gender, age, educational levels, and family status. Those who reside outside North America are more likely to be male (Exhibit 8.2), and they are younger (Exhibit 8.3) and more highly educated (Exhibit 8.4). They are slightly less likely to be married but more likely to have children at home (results not shown). Those within the United States are the most likely to have family members who volunteer: 81.3 percent of respondents in the United States report immediate family members who volunteer, compared to 75.6 percent from Canada or Mexico, and 53.6 percent from countries outside North America (Exhibit 8.5).

EXHIBIT 8.2

Gender by Location

	United States	Canada and Mexico	Outside North America
	%	%	%
Male	53.3	76.8	87.8
Female	46.7	23.2	12.2

EXHIBIT 8.3

Generation by Location

	United States	Canada and Mexico	Outside North America
	%	%	%
Pre-war (1945 or before)	9.1	5.7	5.4
Early Boom (1946–1954)	26.8	21.9	16.3
Late Boom (1955–1962)	30.2	29.8	20.8
Gen X (1963–1976)	28.1	35.7	43.8
Millennials (1977 or later)	5.7	6.8	13.7

EXHIBIT 8.4

Which of the following best describes your highest level of education?

	United States	Canada and Mexico	Outside North America
	%	%	%
High school or less	2.9	4.1	2.0
Some college	5.9	10.0	4.0
Associate degree or equivalent	7.8	10.0	4.9
Bachelor's degree or equivalent	30.8	35.6	33.9
Master's degree or equivalent	33.9	25.7	36.5
PhD, JD, EdD, or equivalent	8.2	7.1	17.8
MD or DDS	10.5	7.5	0.8

EXHIBIT 8.5

Does at least one other member of your immediate family (parents, siblings, spouse, or children) currently engage in volunteer activity or have they done so in the past?

	United States	Canada and Mexico	Outside North America
	%	%	%
Yes	81.3	75.6	53.6
No	17.1	21.9	41.3
Not applicable/no immediate family members	1.6	2.4	5.0

Comparing Volunteering Levels by Region

When we turn to volunteer activity, we begin to see the expected geographical differences, where those outside the United States are less involved in volunteering generally. While in the United States, just 6.1 percent of respondents have never volunteered, the figure increases to 11.3 percent for those in Canada and Mexico and to 27.4 percent for those in other countries (Exhibit 8.6). However, among just the volunteers, individuals outside the United States contribute the same amount of time as those within the United States (Exhibit 8.7). They volunteer for fewer organizations (Exhibit 8.8). Comparing the volunteers, those in the United States are more likely to be involved in civic and community service, educational and youth organizations, and health and religious organizations (Exhibit 8.9). Outside the United States, respondents are more oriented toward professional, technical, or trade organizations. Those in Canada and Mexico are strongly oriented toward sports, hobby, cultural, or arts organizations.

EXHIBIT 8.6

Have you ever worked as a volunteer through or for any organization?

	United States	Canada and Mexico	Outside North America
	%	%	%
In the last 12 months	79.2	70.7	53.9
In the past but not in the last 12 months	14.7	18.0	18.7
Never volunteered	6.1	11.3	27.4

EXHIBIT 8.7

Approximately how many total hours did you perform volunteer work for all the organizations you volunteered for in the last 12 months?
Only for those who have volunteered.

	United States	Canada and Mexico	Outside North America
	%	%	%
1–12 hours	12.3	11.2	11.7
13–49 hours	28.3	27.2	30.3
50–99 hours	25.0	27.0	23.9
100–249 hours	22.1	22.2	22.7
250–499 hours	7.7	8.2	7.0
500 or more hours	4.6	4.2	4.3

EXHIBIT 8.8

For how many different organizations did you perform volunteer work in the last 12 months?

	United States	Canada and Mexico	Outside North America
	%	%	%
One	18.0	24.8	30.5
Two	30.9	35.0	37.1
Three	28.8	25.8	20.5
Four	12.8	9.7	7.0
Five or more	9.5	4.7	4.8

EXHIBIT 8.9

Which of the following best describes the type(s) of organizations for which you volunteered in the last 12 months?
Respondent checked all applicable.

	United States		Canada and Mexico		Outside North America	
	%	Rank	%	Rank	%	Rank
Civic, community service	49.4	1	33.6	3	24.9	3
Religious	47.2	2	24.4	5	20.7	5
Educational or youth service	41.8	3	30.6	4	32.5	2
Professional, technical, or trade	41.1	4	48.3	1	56.6	1
Sport, hobby, cultural, or arts	26.2	5	37.1	2	22.4	4
Nonprofit health organization other than a hospital or clinic	15.1	6	12.1	6	8.5	6
Hospital or clinic	9.1	7	6.8	7	3.0	10
Environmental or animal care	6.6	8	5.6	8	6.4	7
Political group or party	5.5	9	5.3	9	3.8	8
Public safety	4.2	10	3.6	10	3.6	9

Although the lower numbers of volunteers outside the United States suggest that associations will have to work harder to engage these members in volunteering, we are encouraged to find that those outside the United States contribute an equal number of hours and have a stronger interest in professional activities. We also find that they are more likely to report volunteering to contribute their workplace skills (Exhibit 8.10). And members from different geographic areas are not considerably different from one other in reporting a generally positive effect of volunteering on their careers (Exhibit 8.11). In all, we think this represents good news for associations wishing to recruit volunteers from outside the United States.

EXHIBIT 8.10

When you volunteer, do you ever actively seek opportunities to contribute your workplace skills?

	United States	Canada and Mexico	Outside North America
	%	%	%
Yes	71.9	68.7	78.5
No	28.1	31.3	21.5

EXHIBIT 8.11

What effect do you think volunteering has had on your career or, if you are self-employed, on your business?

	United States	Canada and Mexico	Outside North America
	%	%	%
Very negative	0.1	0.0	0.3
2	0.8	1.7	1.0
3	15.2	14.4	19.6
4	29.3	34.0	33.0
Very positive	54.6	50.0	46.0

Volunteer Motivations

Comparing respondents on the perceived benefits of volunteering, we find some distinct differences in how they rank the value of volunteering (Exhibit 8.13, on the following page). Association members from outside North America are similar to those within North America in terms of the relative value they assign to each of the six dimensions, but they are less likely to agree with questions related to helping others (the Values dimension) and more likely to agree with the career-related reasons for volunteering (the Career dimension). However, we have not controlled for gender, which might influence the lower rankings from outside the United States. Within the Understanding dimension, members from outside North America seem particularly more interested in acquiring new skills than those within North America. Respondents from Canada and Mexico have lower scores than members from other nations on many questions.

Volunteering for the Cosponsor

This section examines association volunteering by comparing the frequency of cosponsor volunteering and the choice of activities across regions. We find first that cosponsor members based in the United States are only slightly more likely to be cosponsor volunteers. According to Exhibit 8.12, a total of 45.5 percent of United States members are currently volunteering for a cosponsor or have in the past, compared to 40.1 percent in Canada or Mexico and 41.6 percent outside of North America. Members located outside North America are more likely to be currently volunteering for their cosponsoring organization (37.6 percent) when compared to United

EXHIBIT 8.12

Volunteering for Cosponsor

	United States	Canada and Mexico	Outside North America
	%	%	%
Yes, within the last 12 months	36.4	31.7	37.6
Yes, but longer than 12 months ago	9.1	8.4	4.0
No	54.4	59.9	58.4

EXHIBIT 8.13

Volunteer Functions Inventory (VFI)*

Regardless of your previous volunteer experience, how important or accurate would the following statements be for you in doing volunteer work?

By Location

VFI Dimensions		United States		Canada and Mexico		Outside North America	
		Volunteering in general	Volunteering for cosponsor	Volunteering in general	Volunteering for cosponsor	Volunteering in general	Volunteering for cosponsor
		Mean	Mean	Mean	Mean	Mean	Mean
Values	I feel it is important to help others	4.41	3.91	4.19	3.57	4.09	3.81
	I can do something for a profession or cause that is important to me	4.15	3.96	3.96	3.73	3.85	3.79
	I feel compassion toward people in need	4.13	3.55	3.74	3.04	3.68	3.36
Understanding	Volunteering allows me to gain a new perspective on things	3.88	3.40	3.79	3.28	3.83	3.59
	I can explore my own strengths	3.40	3.22	3.39	3.19	3.56	3.45
	I can learn new skills through direct, hands-on experience	3.35	3.22	3.43	3.26	3.57	3.54
Enhancement	Volunteering makes me feel needed	3.20	2.73	2.91	2.47	3.01	2.92
	Volunteering brings me satisfaction or recognition that I do not get at work	3.13	2.65	2.94	2.56	3.12	3.01
Career	I can make new contacts that might help my business or career	2.67	2.85	2.72	2.94	2.99	3.22
	Volunteer experience looks good on my resume	2.34	2.46	2.42	2.55	2.59	2.85
	Volunteering helps me to explore different career options	2.19	2.33	2.32	2.42	2.75	2.89
	Volunteering gives a competitive advantage to my business	2.16	2.37	2.21	2.41	2.47	2.88
	Volunteering can help me get my foot in the door at a place where I would like to work	1.97	2.18	2.06	2.26	2.52	2.74
Social	Volunteering is important to the people I respect	3.30	3.09	3.20	2.92	3.25	3.12
Protective	Volunteering helps me deal with some of my own problems	2.27	2.04	2.28	2.09	2.67	2.63

*The VFI compares volunteers according to what they believe they gain through volunteer work. Mean shows the average rating on a 1–5 scale with 5=very important. The 15 questions were rated by respondents twice in the survey. First, all respondents were asked about "volunteering in general." Later in the survey, the same questions were asked of respondents who currently volunteer for the cosponsor OR who have volunteered for the cosponsor anytime in the past. Items are grouped according to the six underlying dimensions identified in the Volunteer Functions Inventory (see Bibliography: Clary, Snyder, and Stukas 1996).

States, Canadian or Mexican members. For those members who have volunteered for the cosponsor in the past, those from outside the United States are more likely to have been recent past volunteers (not shown). This finding is important to note since it may be easier to re-engage these lapsed volunteers if they volunteered recently.

Exhibit 8.14 compares hours of service donated by members to cosponsor activities. While the generally low number of hours that all members contribute to their associations is still in evidence, when they volunteer, those located outside North America perform more hours on behalf of the cosponsor than do members within the United States and those from Canada and Mexico. Does this reflect a greater orientation of these non-United States members toward professional volunteering, the availability of fewer competing alternatives, or something else? Whatever the cause, the story that seems to be unfolding is of a willing and particularly valuable but perhaps slightly underutilized membership cohort from outside the United States in terms of their volunteering capacity.

EXHIBIT 8.14

On average, how many hours did you perform volunteer work for [cosponsor] in the last 12 months?

	United States	Canada and Mexico	Outside North America
	%	%	%
1–12 hours	58.7	48.1	43.4
13–49 hours	26.1	30.5	28.5
50–99 hours	9.7	12.9	14.3
100–249 hours	3.8	5.2	10.4
250–499 hours	1.1	3.3	1.5
500 or more hours	0.5	0.0	1.9

Exhibits 8.15 and 8.16 describe the activities that members provide across regions. As expected, given the geographic need, members from outside the United States are more likely to be involved in virtual, or online, volunteering: 26.5 percent in Canada or Mexico, 31.2 percent in other nations outside North America, compared to 17.6 percent in the United States.

Comparing the activities in which members are involved (Exhibit 8.16), we find few regional differences. Those in the United States are more likely to be involved in fundraising, and those in Canada or Mexico are slightly less involved in governance activities. Those outside of North America are more likely to participate in paper or proposal reviews and publication, development of proposals and business plans, standards review, and legislative testimony. Members from outside the United States and Canada or Mexico are also slightly more likely to be engaged in ad hoc rather than formal activities for the cosponsor (21.6 percent in ad hoc activities compared to 17–19 percent for those in North America; not shown). We note that those outside the United States are slightly more likely to work at a senior career level, and this difference may explain some of the volunteer choices.

EXHIBIT 8.15

Have you performed any volunteer work for [cosponsor] by "virtual volunteering," e.g. volunteer activities that are completed, in whole or in part, via the Internet on a home, work, or public access computer?

	United States	Canada and Mexico	Outside North America
	%	%	%
Yes	17.6	26.5	31.2
No	82.4	73.5	68.8

In terms of how they were recruited into volunteering, we see some geographic differences (Exhibit 8.17). Respondents from Canada or Mexico were more likely than those from the United States or outside North America to have volunteered for their association at a meeting or local chapter and also more likely to have taken the initiative and contacted the organization themselves or to have been asked by another volunteer. Members from outside North America were more likely to have been asked by association staff or to have responded to a web site posting.

EXHIBIT 8.16

In the last 12 months, have you done any of the following as a volunteer (in person, online, or in any other way) on behalf of [cosponsor]?

Respondent checked all applicable.

	United States		Canada and Mexico		Outside North America	
	%	Rank	%	Rank	%	Rank
Provided mentoring, coaching, or tutoring for members, students, or others	14.4	1	13.0	1	12.8	2
Provided professional advice	13.4	2	11.2	3	13.2	1
Recruited a member or members	12.4	3	11.3	2	12.0	3
Served on a committee for a local chapter or section	11.1	4	8.6	5	8.7	8
Participated in a discussion group, expert panel, or report	8.6	5	8.0	6	10.0	7
Spoke or presented a paper	8.5	6	9.1	4	11.7	4
Served on the board for a local chapter or section	7.3	7	5.8	8	7.2	11
Moderated or facilitated discussion groups at meetings or elsewhere	6.3	8	6.5	7	7.5	10
Raised funds	6.2	9	3.0	15	3.7	16
Reviewed a paper or proposal for a publication	5.4	10	4.9	9	10.4	6
Submitted a paper or manuscript for publication	4.6	11	4.8	10	10.6	5
Served on a committee for the parent organization	4.6	12	3.5	14	4.1	15
Served on a technical committee or reviewed standards and practices	4.3	13	4.3	11	7.2	12
Reviewed proposals for conferences or projects	4.2	14	4.3	12	8.1	9
Reviewed research, conducted literature review or resource reviews or analyzed data	4.1	15	4.1	13	5.7	13
Reviewed applications as part of accreditation, certification, or competitive program	3.2	16	2.4	16	3.3	17
Wrote proposals, grant applications, or business plans	2.7	17	2.4	17	4.4	14
Made a presentation or testified on behalf of the organization to any legislative body (local, state, national, or global advocacy)	2.3	18	1.6	18	3.2	18
Served on the board for the parent organization	1.6	19	1.5	19	1.3	20
Prepared background for regulators, the press, or others	1.5	20	1.0	20	2.5	19

EXHIBIT 8.17

How did you first learn about the volunteer opportunities available to you through [cosponsor]?
Respondent selected only one.

	United States		Canada and Mexico		Outside North America	
	%	Rank	%	Rank	%	Rank
I don't recall	26.6	1	22.0	1	29.5	1
Through a local chapter or section	14.5	2	15.2	2	10.3	4
At a meeting, conference, or other event	13.6	3	14.9	3	10.5	3
I was asked by another volunteer	13.3	4	14.9	4	10.5	2
A staff member of the organization asked me to volunteer	8.9	5	6.0	5	10.0	5
Through my employer (current or past)	5.2	6	4.6	8	4.0	9
I answered a call/ad for volunteers	5.1	7	5.3	6	5.4	7
Through a professor or someone at my university or school	3.7	8	3.2	11	3.1	10
Through a posting on their web site	2.7	10	3.5	9	7.8	6
I contacted the organization and offered to volunteer	2.7	9	5.0	7	2.9	11
I saw an advertisement in the organization's magazine or other publication	2.1	11	3.5	10	4.3	8
Other way	1.6	12	1.8	12	1.6	12

Satisfaction With Volunteering for a Cosponsor

When we compare cosponsor volunteers on the question of satisfaction with volunteering, we find that those from outside North America are the most satisfied overall with cosponsor volunteering (Exhibit 8.18). Among association members, 60 percent are satisfied or very satisfied with cosponsor volunteering, compared to 54.8 percent for those in the United States and 53.1 percent for those in Canada and Mexico. The Canadian/Mexican group was also most likely to indicate they were dissatisfied with volunteering but otherwise had responses quite similar to those of the United States.

We see the same pattern when we look at the likelihood of continuing to volunteer for the cosponsor or of recommending cosponsor volunteering to a friend or colleague in Exhibits 8.19 and 8.20. Again, cosponsor volunteers from outside North America are substantially more satisfied with volunteering. However, when asked how satisfied they were with specific aspects of their volunteer experience with a cosponsor, responses were similar across geographic boundaries (results not shown).

EXHIBIT 8.18

Please use the scale provided below to rate your overall satisfaction with volunteering for [cosponsor].

	United States	Canada and Mexico	Outside North America
	%	%	%
Very dissatisfied	1.7	1.5	2.4
2	6.7	8.5	4.7
3	36.7	36.9	32.9
4	35.8	38.1	43.3
Very satisfied	19.0	15.0	16.7

EXHIBIT 8.19

How likely is it that you will be a volunteer for [cosponsor] within the next 12 months?

	United States	Canada and Mexico	Outside North America
	%	%	%
Very unlikely	28.5	30.6	20.1
2	21.6	24.2	15.1
3	25.4	21.0	26.5
4	11.6	11.6	18.0
Very likely	12.8	12.6	20.3

EXHIBIT 8.20

How likely is it that you would recommend volunteering for [cosponsor] to a friend or colleague?

	United States	Canada and Mexico	Outside North America
	%	%	%
Very unlikely	19.9	19.5	14.4
2	18.3	20.7	15.8
3	31.1	28.6	28.2
4	17.2	18.4	22.1
Very likely	13.4	12.7	19.6

Ample Opportunities Outside the United States

Throughout this study we have observed that most United States-based association members who volunteer do so for multiple organizations. As a result, a crowding out effect is evident in the substantially fewer hours that members devote to association volunteering when compared to community volunteering—particularly when they are parents. What we find, however, when we compare members across countries is that members outside the United States are possibly less subject to this effect. The greater orientation of members outside the United States toward professional volunteering could be due to the fewer voluntary organizations that compete for members' time or simply to their natural inclination. Whatever the cause, there are ample opportunities for associations to call on members outside the United States for volunteer help and plenty of members willing to help—provided associations understand how to engage them effectively.

There also appear to be some barriers to international volunteering. We did not produce a sufficiently focused examination to understand the extent of the challenge, but it is clear that some members find geography a barrier. One member wrote, "I am residing in India, and I would like to get actively involved in [cosponsor] activities. Mere geographical location should not be the reason to disqualify me." Another wrote, "I appreciate your efforts [since the country I live in] doesn't have a 'culture' of volunteer activity."

Others expressed frustration: "I do not know how to support [cosponsor] from Europe…China…Australia…and so on." And finally, some assume that geography is a barrier, whether or not it actually is: "I am unwilling to consider volunteering at this time, as I will be moving to a new overseas assignment."

As for clues on how to manage volunteers outside the United States, we found little difference across geographic boundaries when examining specific sources of satisfaction or dissatisfaction with membership volunteering (such as feedback, incentives, recognition). We did find some difference with respect to the perceived benefits of volunteering, but these differences do not indicate that non-United States volunteers are substantially less motivated than those in the United States. This suggests that members think in pretty similar terms about the benefits of volunteering. The question for you and your volunteer program, then, is whether you are serving volunteers from different geographic regions with the same level of support. If your association membership has a strong international representation and you are interested in the issues we raise in this chapter, you might survey your members on the quality of those volunteer management practices that are most dependent on distance and geography such as training, leadership opportunities, and opportunities to work and socialize with peers.

There are ample opportunities for associations to call on members outside the United States for volunteer help, and plenty of members willing to help—provided associations understand how to engage them effectively.

Geography

The findings in THE DECISION TO VOLUNTEER are fodder for thought with respect to the need for sensitivity to the cultural norms, orientation toward volunteerism, and practical considerations present among membership pools outside of the United States. Depending on the makeup of your organization's pool of prospects, members and nonmembers outside of the United States may represent significant opportunities for engagement. Consider these questions among others:

- How does the geography of volunteering manifest itself in your organization? What information do you need to obtain from your members to understand how their location influences their volunteer options? What adjustments could you make to your volunteer recruitment strategies, volunteer tasks, and volunteer support, to increase participation by certain geographic groups?

- What are the cultural norms for volunteering in the countries where your members and volunteers live and work? What does your organization do to address your volunteer marketing messages to members outside of the United States?

- For those volunteers who relocate to areas where it is harder to obtain some volunteering benefits (such as socializing and networking), can you find alternative ways to provide those benefits?

- How can you capitalize on the stronger interest in professional volunteer activities expressed by many international members?

- Do you use different recruitment techniques for your international members or those who have recently moved to the United States? Should you?

- Have you developed specific volunteer opportunities or tasks for your international members?

- This study suggests that the greater orientation of members outside the United States toward professional volunteering could be due to the fewer voluntary organizations that compete for members' time. How can your organization maximize the opportunity to recruit from this pool of available and willing volunteers?

- What can you learn from your member volunteers outside of North America regarding their satisfaction with the volunteer experience that can translate to increased satisfaction of all your volunteers?

CHAPTER 9

Reaching the Non-Volunteer

WITH ALL THE ATTENTION paid by practitioners and scholars alike to *volunteers*, it is instructive to remember that three quarters of Americans do *not* volunteer. Why not? As we have explored in this book, *upbringing* and *opportunity* both play a role. Upbringing, through examples set by family, employers, and community members, socialize individuals into and out of volunteering. For every individual who believes that part of a successful life is giving back to the community, another believes in being paid for his or her labor. Opportunities for volunteering are created when people have the time, good health, and financial wherewithal to serve and are restricted when family, financial, or professional responsibilities limit free time. Opportunity also describes the ways in which public and private institutions create a need for volunteers and then support volunteerism with effective programs and policies. Among the non-volunteers in our study we expect to find many who have tried volunteering but haven't found it to be a positive experience. Our job is to help associations understand how to avoid those pitfalls.

An interesting fact about volunteers is that they can start volunteering for one reason and stick around for another. In this chapter, we explore not only the rationales people offer for never volunteering but also those for ending a volunteer role; this distinction matters. People may be drawn to a cause, a need, or an opportunity to make a difference on an issue that matters to them, but the perceived benefits of their volunteer experience might come from another source entirely: the opportunity to learn something new, strengthen skills, build a social network, receive training, or enjoy status and public recognition. It takes organizational resources to understand what benefits volunteers expect to receive and to ensure that they get them. And that means that successful volunteers are created not only by their own initiative but by the organizations that help them reap the benefits of volunteering.

> **Successful volunteers are created not only by their own initiative but by the organizations that help them reap the benefits of volunteering.**

We introduced in Chapter 2 the notion of the controllable and uncontrollable reasons why people enter and exit volunteering, or never volunteer at all. The bounds between what is controllable and what is not are open to debate, but we suggest that many of the questions we posed to non-volunteers about why they did not volunteer can be addressed through effective programs and policies. At the end of this chapter, we will offer some specific suggestions.

Organization of This Chapter

This chapter has three sections. We first describe the reasons that our survey participants provided for not volunteering at all (7.8 percent of all respondents). These individuals were asked 17 follow-up questions, posed as a set of strategies that might get people involved in volunteering.[1] The second section of this chapter describes the respondents' explanation of why they did not volunteer for the cosponsor in particular (54.9 percent of all respondents). These 20 questions were posed to any respondent who did not volunteer for a cosponsor association and are written with association volunteering in mind. The final section of this chapter uses the words of our survey respondents to put into context the reasons that association members provide for not volunteering. Here we also offer suggestions on how associations can address these barriers to volunteering.

Why Individuals Do Not Volunteer

In Exhibit 9.1, the 17 possible reasons we offered individuals for why they might not volunteer at all are listed in rank order according to the level of agreement with the question. The higher the number on a scale of 1 (strongly disagree) to 5 (strongly agree) the more our respondents agreed with that reason. In the columns on the right of the table, selected demographic characteristics of our respondents are displayed (their age, gender, etc.). A plus sign indicates that a respondent with that characteristic agrees more with the question, holding all other characteristics constant. A minus sign indicates that respondents with that characteristic disagree more with the question. A blank indicates that no statistically significant relationship was found on the demographic condition listed.

The most strongly supported barriers to volunteering that non-volunteers expressed were:

1. Not finding a meaningful opportunity
2. Not having the right skills
3. Not having an accessible location

Respondents agreed with all questions more than they disagreed (scores of 3 or higher) with the exception of the last one, reimbursement for expenses. What seems to matter the most is finding a volunteer opportunity that has meaning for them, and that they can manage around their other responsibilities.

When respondent demographic characteristics were included in the analysis (the set of columns in Exhibit 9.1), we find that older respondents seem to be more concerned about having the right skills and more likely to have had a past poor experience with volunteering. Generally, however, they are less likely to agree with any of the other reasons, which we interpret to mean that older non-volunteers may be just less willing to start volunteering at their age. Women, on the other hand, appear to be more willing since they agree more strongly with most of the reasons we provided. Reading across the next three columns, we find a mixed bag for those with family members who volunteer, children, and higher educations. They

---

[1] Surprisingly, we found that some who said they did not volunteer went on in the course of the survey to describe at least one way in which they actually did serve their cosponsor organization. We have included their responses here anyway, but we note that some who consider themselves non-volunteers actually do volunteer for the cosponsor, although they do not volunteer in their non-professional lives.

EXHIBIT 9.1

People who do not currently volunteer for any organization report:
"I would start volunteering now if:"

	Mean response in order of agreement	Respondent characteristics that increase (+) or decrease (-) agreement with the survey question							
		Older age	Female	Family volunteers	Children at home	Higher education	Live in Canada/ Mexico	Live outside North America	Self employed
I knew the volunteer opportunity was meaningful or made a difference in people's lives	4.29		+	+					
I knew I had the skills needed to do a good job	4.06	+	+	+				+	
The location was easily accessible to me	3.93	−	+						−
I was interested in volunteering	3.90		+				+		
I did not lose income as a result	3.90	−	+			−			−
I could be given short-term assignments	3.77	−	+						
I had more information about volunteer opportunities available to me	3.57	−	+			−			
A volunteer organization would train me to do the work	3.55	−	+			−			−
My employer supported my participation as a volunteer	3.48	−						−	
I knew it would make a difference to my profession or in my work	3.45	−	+	−					
I was actually asked to volunteer	3.37	−						−	
I knew someone else who also worked or volunteered there	3.34	−	−	−	−			−	
I could volunteer electronically or virtually	3.32	−	+	−		+		+	
I was recognized and appreciated for my work as a volunteer	3.31								
I was not disappointed with volunteering in the past	3.28	+					+	+	
The organization that needed help was one that had, in the past, helped me or someone I love	3.25	−	+					−	−
I was reimbursed for expenses such as meals or gas allowance	2.68	−		−			+	+	

NOTE: The scores in column 2 reflect the average responses to this question from all members who indicated in that they do not volunteer at all now. Responses were on a scale of 1–5 with 5=strongly agree. The remaining columns reflect the influence of various demographic factors on a respondent's likelihood of agreeing to each question. The results were produced via regression analysis. A "+" indicates that respondents with the characteristic are more likely to agree with the question, holding other factors constant. A "−" indicates that respondents with the characteristic are less likely to agree with that question. Blank fields indicate that no statistically significant relationship was found. Statistically significant relationships are reported at 95% or greater confidence.

are less likely to agree with a few of reasons for starting to volunteer, but the connection is not strong. We note in particular that respondents who have family who volunteer (the majority of our sample) are more drawn to opportunities with meaning, and those with a higher education are more drawn to virtual volunteering.

Looking at respondents from outside the United States, those in Canada or Mexico appear less likely to be interested in volunteering, more likely to have been disappointed in the past, and more likely to expect reimbursement. Those outside North America are more concerned about having the right skills, less concerned about employer support for volunteering (an encouraging finding), and more likely to look for virtual volunteering opportunities.

We pulled one career-related characteristic from our variables to analyze. Those who are self-employed are less concerned about accessibility, losing income (another surprising connection), and less concerned about training.

Reasons for Not Volunteering for the Cosponsor

All of our respondents are current members of a cosponsor organization, but most have not volunteered for that association (54.9 percent) and some (8.7 percent) have stopped volunteering for a cosponsor. Just over one third (36.4 percent) of the respondents currently volunteer for a cosponsor, although three quarters have recent community volunteer experience (see Exhibit 3.13).

Just one third of the members in our full sample currently volunteer for a cosponsor, although three quarters have recent community volunteer experience.

This section of the chapter looks at the association members who are not current volunteers—they have volunteered for a cosponsor in the past, or never volunteered. But many who have never volunteered for the cosponsor have volunteered elsewhere. Very few in this group are individuals who have never volunteered anywhere.

Exhibit 9.2 shows the reasons provided by those who do not volunteer for the cosponsor, in order of frequency. This table also displays the results of the same kind of statistical analysis performed in Exhibit 9.1, using demographic characteristics of the respondents to predict greater or lesser agreement with a reason.

The most commonly cited reason for not volunteering for the cosponsor, expressed by 38.7 percent of the respondents, is lack of information about opportunities to volunteer. The second most frequent reason is a conflict with some other volunteering activity (35.1 percent), and the third is not having been asked to volunteer (28.7 percent). At least one in five respondents also reported not knowing about virtual volunteering opportunities (23 percent) or short-term assignments (22.4 percent). Agreement with other reasons begins to drop off considerably from this point onward, suggesting a great amount of consistency in which reasons respondents considered most important. We note, for example, that more than half (53.7 percent) of the respondents at the entry-level in the career ladder agreed with the first question, "I do not have enough information about volunteer opportunities available to me" (not shown).

The most commonly cited reason for not volunteering for the cosponsor is lack of information about opportunities to volunteer.

Older volunteers are more likely to report that they volunteer elsewhere, find the location inconvenient, do not have their employer's support, do not have the skills or training, or have had an offer to volunteer rejected by the cosponsor. They are less likely to lack the information or to have been asked, to be interested in virtual volunteering or short-term assignments, and to know others who volunteer. We find the association between age and training noteworthy since we might assume that older volunteers actually have more skills. But these results suggest that they feel at a disadvantage in many associations as skills change. In your own association, you might try asking some more targeted questions of these members about their technical skills and training related to computers.

We will remark on just a few other interesting associations here. We find women to be particularly interested in virtual volunteering and short-term assignments. This connection may be due to greater family responsibilities. We find again that family and educational status influences agreement with questions in both positive and negative directions. As predicted, those

EXHIBIT 9.2

Which of the following best describes why you do not currently volunteer for [cosponsor] now?

Asked of respondents who have never volunteered for a cosponsor and of those who have volunteered for a cosponsor in the past but do not do so now.

	Mean response in order of agreement	Respondent characteristics that increase (+) or decrease (-) agreement with the survey question									
		Older age	Female	Family volunteers	Children at home	More education	Live in Canada/ Mexico	Live outside North America	Self employed	More years in profession	More years as a member
I do not have enough information about volunteer opportunities available to me.	38.7%	−	+	−	−					−	−
I volunteer elsewhere.	35.1%	+	−	+	+	−		−	+	+	+
They never asked me to volunteer.	28.7%	−	−	−	−	−	−			+	−
I do not know of any volunteer opportunities that can be done electronically or virtually.	23.0%	−	+	−	−	−		+		−	−
I do not know of any short-term assignments for volunteers.	22.4%	−	+	−	−	−					−
The location is inconvenient for me.	16.3%	+	+	+		+	+	+	−		+
I do not know anyone who works or volunteers for them.	15.0%	−	−		−	+	−			−	−
I am not interested in volunteering for them.	11.5%					+		−	+		+
My employer does not support it.	5.0%	+	−						−		+
I do not think volunteering for them would make a difference in my profession or work.	4.9%		−		−	+				+	
I am concerned about losing income as a result.	4.8%			−		+			+	−	
I do not have the training necessary to volunteer for them.	4.3%	+	+	−			+	+		−	−
I do not have the skills needed to do a good job.	3.4%	+				+		+		−	
They do not reimburse volunteers for expenses like travel or meals.	2.6%			−					−		
I have been disappointed with volunteering for them in the past.	1.6%					−					+
They do not offer enough opportunities for volunteers to network with one another.	1.5%					−		+		−	
They didn't accept my offer to volunteer.	1.4%	+	−			−					
Term limits or other policy adopted by the organization prevents me from volunteering now.	0.8%							+	−		
They do not recognize and appreciate the work of volunteers.	0.6%										
Volunteering is not supported in my country.	0.6%						+	+			

NOTE: The scores in column 2 reflect the average responses to this question from all members who indicated in Question 2 that they do not volunteer. The answers were scaled from 1 (strongly disagree) to 5 (strongly agree). The higher the number, the more likely the full sample agreed with this question. The remaining columns reflect the influence of various factors on a respondent's likelihood of agreeing to each question. The results were produced via logistic regression analysis. A "+" indicates that respondents with the characteristic are more likely to agree with the question, holding other factors constant. A "−" indicates that respondents with the characteristic are less likely to agree with that question.

with children were more likely to indicate that they volunteer elsewhere. The lesson here is not to assume that those who have the socio-economic profile we look for when we recruit volunteers will all behave in the same way regarding incentives or recruitment methods. For example, although we find those with advanced degrees to be less likely to say they have been disappointed with cosponsor volunteering in the past, they are also just slightly more likely to say they are not interested in volunteering for the cosponsor.

This pattern of responses is something that each association should be able to act on, depending on the makeup of your membership base. You may wish, for example, to work harder at structuring volunteer responsibilities so that they do not compete with other professional responsibilities, and you may also wish to develop more opportunities for men or women who are occupied with family responsibilities to engage in short-term and long-distance or Internet-based volunteer opportunities. Desktop publishing, manuscript review, member recruitment, research, blogging, distance training, web site support, and even fundraising can, to some extent, be accomplished through virtual volunteering (Murray and Harrison 2005).

We find the profile of those outside North America to be particularly encouraging with respect to future volunteer recruitment. These individuals are less likely to volunteer elsewhere, more interested in virtual volunteering, more interested in volunteering for a cosponsor, and more interested in networking. However, they are also more likely to find the location inconvenient, more concerned about having the right skills to volunteer, and—because they seem to be called upon to represent their associations more actively overseas—more likely to be up against term limits.

Finally, when we examine some career-related characteristics of our respondents, we find that those who have been in their professions longer, and those who have been association members longer, seem more informed about volunteer opportunities but also more likely to have had a bad experience in the past. We note in particular that on the third question, "They never asked me to volunteer," there is a disconnect where only those who have been members longer have been asked to volunteer more. This means that there are many members who have been in the profession for years but perhaps have not been members of your association for as long, and subsequently haven't been asked to volunteer. New members can bring a wealth of experience if they have been in the profession for a long time. If you keep records on how long your members have been in their respective professions, you may be able to tap this source of expertise for some new volunteers.

Association Practices that Discourage Volunteers

In these survey questions and in the open-ended question we asked of all members, we found several themes that point to specific ways in which associations discourage members from volunteering. All of the following barriers to volunteering can be addressed, in our opinion. We list them along with some suggestions on how to tackle them if you find it worthwhile to do so in your organization.

Just Fill Out a Form

Some respondents described volunteer recruitment methods that were ineffective because they were not visible, staff-supported, or actively marketed to members. For example:

> *I have never been contacted about volunteering and I only knew it was an option by a brief mention of it in an email recently.*

> *I have consistently looked for volunteer activities with [cosponsor]…without success. If opportunities were out there beyond filling out the on-line form then I haven't found them.*

> *I've expressed my interest to volunteer twice through the web site and both times, never got a proper communication whether my service is required except for an automated reply.*

> *I have never felt [cosponsor] volunteer opportunities to be visible or accessible. Other organizations have calls for participation, open calls for authors for newsletters, and open calls for speakers as entry-level volunteer opportunities.*

Suggestions: Depending on how important volunteers are to your organization, passive recruitment strategies may not be effective in getting you what you want. Some strategies for giving volunteer opportunities a higher profile in your organization include setting up a volunteer booth at meetings, regular open calls for participation, peer-to-peer recruitment, multiple rather than single recruitment methods to reach different audiences, and effective use of the web site and email communication. An important element in this marketing package is visibility for the work that volunteers accomplish:

> *I would like to see more of the volunteers' backgrounds and history of service mentioned in [cosponsor] journals so members get to know our volunteers. I also think that this may encourage other members to volunteer when they discover how much alike we are.*

Lack of Follow Through

We received numerous comments from members like the following:

> *I have called [cosponsor] several times to try to volunteer for them and was told I was not needed.*

> *I called to volunteer to go to Washington, D.C. to meet with my senators and no one called me back; thus I never went.*

Members also told us they responded when asked to volunteer but still received no follow-up from association staff or members:

> *I have volunteered several times…by responding to ads and talking to colleagues. I have never been asked (or had any follow-up regarding my inquiries) to serve.*

> *I volunteered through the web site or to be a [peer review, mentor, committee member] and nobody ever contacted me.*

> *I would love to get involved with [cosponsor] and I have tried repeatedly. I was told to sign up and have never heard anything back.*

> *It would be nice to know when you are not selected for a volunteer position. One volunteers and then never hears back.*

Suggestions: There are really two things going on here: Your association may not have a strong enough need for a formal volunteer program, so that those who volunteer cannot be effectively involved. If so, you must at least develop a means of involving those you do need (such as board members) and you must still communicate to those you don't need to thank them for their support. If you don't, members will associate the lack of follow-through with poor membership services.

If you do have a formal volunteer program and regular needs for volunteers, following up on offers of help is even more essential. The essential elements of volunteer management include recordkeeping, effective matching of needs and skills (which can sometimes involve job descriptions), orientation or training, support, evaluation, and recognition. All of these elements involve establishing a long-term relationship with a volunteer that depends on professionality. The easiest way to signal to prospective volunteers that you really don't need them is to ignore them or take them for granted:

> **When members check the blank on the renewal form that they are willing to volunteer, RESPOND.**

Pay Your Own Way

Numerous members commented on the financial cost of volunteering:

> *Policies related to travel and meals were very frugal.*

> *I would like to be more involved [with cosponsor], but the hour drive each way to the nearest chapter is simply too long.*

> *There are too many restrictions on out-of-pocket expense reimbursement for volunteers.*

Although we find in Exhibit 9.1 that reimbursement for expenses is not an important motivation to get non-volunteers involved *initially* in association work, it may be an important way to *keep* them volunteering because expense reimbursement offers a tangible expression of appreciation to volunteers. We found in Exhibit 3.20 that the aspect of the volunteer experience with which association volunteers were least satisfied was receiving incentives like stipends, transportation, or meals. Several members reminded us that they often pay their own way to events and meetings and are not reimbursed by their associations for hotel, mileage, or meals. The IRS allows organizations to reimburse volunteers for the ordinary expenses of volunteering without any risk to exempt status. If the association does not provide the reimbursement, members have only the option of a partial tax deduction (and the volunteer mileage rate provides little incentive to travel, since it is artificially low at $0.14 per mile for 501(c)(3) charitable nonprofits).

Suggestions: Reimbursement may not matter to all of your volunteers, but you should explore its impact on those at the governance level especially for Shapers and other super-volunteers in your organization. Members made the following suggestions: Improve per diem rates, simplify reimbursement procedures, and make the reimbursement policies more equitable between staff and volunteer work. The bottom line is that reimbursement rates must reflect the value that volunteers bring to the organization so that the cost of volunteering does not provide a disincentive to members.

The Unfriendly Skies

We did not see a lot of comments like the following, but they are alarming when they show up:

> *[My association is run by] old boy/old girl, personal, self-appointed and self-perpetuating relationships.*

> *Most of the [cosponsor] stuff I have been to has been boring and unattractive to students and young professionals. And we wonder why very few go into this field.*

> *When I asked what were the duties of a board member I was told, "Just come to the board meetings." I felt I was wasting my time.*

> *I have attended several local meetings. I find the members very unfriendly as they talk amongst themselves and don't welcome new people in.*

> *Staff do not actively encourage…their volunteers.*

Suggestions: New volunteers will have two points of connection in your organization: other volunteers or professional staff. Both of these groups can create problems for your volunteer program if they are unwilling or unprepared to welcome in new volunteers and support their involvement. All staff members who work with volunteers must have a firm grasp on the value that volunteers bring to your organization. It also helps to train staff in effective volunteer involvement so that they understand the different set of incentives under which volunteers operate. Solutions to staff-volunteer

tension (or tension between older and newer volunteers) might also require policies on committee rotation and term limits. Tensions can be reduced by having the board set policies and procedures for volunteer involvement. We highly recommend Susan Ellis's book, *From the Top Down* (1996) for more on this subject. Ellis reminds us that it takes board and executive leadership to fully integrate a volunteer program into your organizational strategies. When staff understands the strategic value of volunteers—and when volunteers understand their connection to the mission—comments like those above should happen less frequently.

Take a Number

Survey respondents told us they sometimes got the message about volunteering in their profession that there was a pecking order driven by experience and credentials. In certain instances, members told us that they did not have a high enough degree to be accepted as a volunteer in their professional association.

> *I [earned my degree] as a second career and do not feel as "expert" as others who have been in the profession all of their careers.*

> *Those of us who are not certified sometimes wonder if we have the credentials to be a legitimate volunteer.*

> *Volunteering for the [cosponsor] is generally for elites.*

> *I am not sure how my knowledge base compares with the other members in the local chapter, since I don't have any of the quality certifications from [cosponsor]. This makes me a bit insecure about…volunteering [for them].*

Suggestions: Associations should clearly communicate to members which credentials are required for which volunteer jobs. When credentials do not matter, associations should consider the value of involving members with less association or professional experience in some decision-making in order to benefit from a more diverse range of perspectives and in order to develop a career ladder for volunteers within the organization. Finally, younger and less experienced members may require additional support to be effective in their volunteer roles such as peer mentoring or targeted messages that guide them toward appropriate tasks and reassure them they have something to offer:

Some people are afraid of failing, so it is good to have them tag along with the current established volunteer.

The Cost-Benefit Factor

Some respondents wrote about their desire to balance their volunteer work with some level of expected benefits. The literature on volunteer recognition from the charitable sector may have limited value here since a dues-based professional association may find that its volunteers expect more tangible forms of recognition and reward than charities ordinarily offer. Even so, to many of our respondents, it was clear that organizations have overlooked the least expensive but potentially most effective form of recognition: a regular and sincere "thank you" to volunteers:

This year, I put in so many hours…that I feel a bit burned out. I felt I should be recognized for my outstanding effort—that doesn't appear to be happening. I don't want to put myself out in the future. Without recognition, for me especially, the sails have lost their wind! Not being honored for my effort offers no incentive, at all, for me to continue volunteering on the same intense level.

I was a bit disappointed that there is no comprehensive training or aids to help a new volunteer/board member get a handle on where and how to best participate on behalf of the membership.

To volunteer time for an organization other than one for the needy, there must be rewards to compensate for the time and effort.

Makes me wonder why I bother to volunteer when all I see are sticks and very few carrots.

As a former local chapter president, I think there should be more formalized acknowledgement of that contribution by at minimum a "thank you" note or certificate of recognition from national which can be shared with an employer. Little things…go a long way to make volunteers feel recognized and appreciated and don't necessarily cost a lot of time or money.

I was a chapter president for two years and received nothing from the main office.

You need to do a better job of appreciating the value of volunteers.

Suggestions: Although plenty of respondents told us that they expected no reciprocation in their volunteer activity, just as many had specific ideas about how they should be rewarded or recognized. Suggestions included access to online association resources in exchange for volunteer hours (a volunteer "credit bank"), training, reimbursement for out-of-pocket expenses, discounted meeting fees or dues, ability to audit courses in exchange for teaching a course, and so on. Members also reminded us that intangible forms of recognition also have value:

The key to coming in and volunteering is how organized and respectful of your time the organization is.

But You Do It So Well…

"I feel like I cannot get out of my current role," wrote one member. Another observed:

Volunteerism is a good thing. I just wish more people would share the responsibility of spreading the word about certain causes and issues. I'm exhausted!

Suggestions: Exit interviews can be used with volunteers to assess the level of burnout in your organization. Depending on the same individuals to accomplish everything can result in the premature loss of some of your best volunteers. Your most successful efforts may come from reaching beyond the usual suspects to bring in fresh talent. This requires a system to identify and cultivate new talent so that the volunteer program gets a new infusion of energy periodically.

Don't Like Membership, Unlikely to Volunteer

The two volumes THE DECISION TO JOIN and THE DECISION TO VOLUNTEER have at least one thing in common: They are both focused upon improving the satisfaction of association members. At the end of the day, members who are unhappy with their membership benefits are less likely to volunteer—and to renew:

I would feel much better about volunteering if [cosponsor] would stop wasting my dues on activities that don't benefit the members.

I would likely volunteer in the next 12 months, but my local chapter is in disarray.

Volunteering for [cosponsor] has been tainted by the national office cutting support for local sections and divisions.

I have asked for help twice from the [cosponsor] and twice I have been ignored.

Why do you need people's free time and dedication when your fees are so steep?

Looking for Balance in Life

Some members are active community volunteers but are unwilling to volunteer for professional activities because they are looking for something else in their volunteer activities:

I look for volunteer opportunities outside of [my profession] for life and family balance. I would rather volunteer at a hospital or somewhere where you would have an effect on someone's happiness. Not stuffing envelopes or working on web sites for the [cosponsor]. Sorry.

My time spent volunteering is not related to my job or career, and I like that separation. There is more to me than being a [professional].

Voluntary work is an important part of life [but] there is more to life than work.

I generally volunteer for humanitarian causes as opposed to work related causes. Not really interested in spending my free time doing work related things.

Suggestions: This is a harder issue for an association to address since it's about a conscious choice that volunteers make about their leisure time. However, depending on your mission, you may be able to steer potential volunteers like these toward activities that have greater social value. These kinds of volunteers may not be good prospects for a technical committee, but they may be interested in social or humanitarian activities, including mentoring new members or working with disadvantaged or underserved populations. You may also be able to attract these kinds of volunteers to your work by offering them opportunities for new experiences they cannot obtain through their professional work.

Concluding Thoughts

It's hard to end a book with the kind of cold, hard dose of reality you find in this chapter. Not all of your members possess a strong enough affiliation with your organization or a strong enough motivation toward professional service to volunteer for you. For some, life intervenes. For others, volunteering for one's professional organization is a busman's holiday, and they deliberately seek out community volunteering rather than association volunteering. For most, any potential volunteer activity is linked solidly to how they feel about their membership benefits, and you won't solve one challenge until you address the other (but that's another book).

The volunteer experience can become a membership benefit of its own.

But we hope you see this chapter as an opportunity as well as a challenge. The opportunity lies in our finding that many members are looking for more ways to connect their professional work to their personal values. For those who *do* volunteer, the single most important reason they offer is that volunteering makes a difference to their profession. The benefits for association volunteers reflect a combination of the self-serving and other-serving reasons behind their effort. Volunteer programs offer members an opportunity to connect their values to their professional work, and to act on a very basic and human need: a chance to support, learn from, and share with peers. In short, as members have told us in this survey, the volunteer experience can become a membership benefit of its own. Witness these comments:

I love volunteering for [cosponsor]. I consider it a benefit of membership.

I have easily gained as much as I have given.

Volunteering is THE reason I belong to the organization.

Volunteering for a national organization gives you a better perspective for the whole 'picture'.

I feel VERY strongly that volunteering has led to opportunities that I never would have had otherwise.

I receive greater "job satisfaction" from my volunteer experience than from work. I also have learned many skills while volunteering that helped me excel in my career.

My volunteer activities taught me more than a business management course about running a meeting, doing a budget, doing strategic planning, and bringing people to consensus.

Volunteering is a great way to meet new people, network, and explore other career opportunities.

I believe there is a strong association between consistent volunteering and overall life satisfaction. Hopefully the results will reveal that professionals taking the time and effort to be a part of a larger purpose are also the professionals with the greatest satisfaction in their personal and professional lives.

If you agree, from your own association perspective, with this notion that volunteering is a membership benefit—and it will only work if your organization believes an investment in volunteer management has strategic value—you will have to invest just as much effort into your volunteer programs as you do in other membership activities.

ACTING ON THE FINDINGS
Why Don't Members Volunteer?

Organizations need to have clear and consistent strategies from the board level about how volunteers support the mission. Without this strategic direction from the top, volunteers will not get the recognition they need, staff will not understand how to work with volunteers effectively, and other volunteers will not recognize the value of helping new volunteers get involved. The suggestions here include additional data collection strategies, but no amount of additional data will overcome the absence of a top-down commitment to effective volunteer management.

Once your organization's leadership has acknowledged the strategic importance of volunteer management, one approach might be to consider using THE DECISION TO VOLUNTEER response options identified in this chapter in a targeted quantitative survey. A second option would be to conduct your own open-ended qualitative research, either through a focus group or open-end survey questions to identify reasons specific to your association. Then follow up with a quantitative survey using your list of frequently cited factors.

Divide the list into two columns to isolate basic factors involving a relatively simple fix from complex factors requiring time and careful attention.

Non-Volunteers in General

Rank	Basic Factors	Complex Factors
1	*Ex.* Unaware of opportunities	*Ex.* Disappointed with past association volunteer experience
2		
3		
4		
5		
6		
7		
8		
9		
10		

The breakdown and ranking of factors will enable your association to identify short-term and long-term priorities for improving your volunteer program and converting non-volunteers to volunteers on both ends of the spectrum.

For greater insight, take the findings above cross-referenced by specific subgroups, such as career stage, family situation, employment environment, world location, or other demographic characteristics that are important to your organization.

As we have learned, non-volunteer audiences differ based upon their own unique factors. One way to create a more tactical volunteer conversion strategy is using a rating based upon intent to volunteer in the future. Rating scores could be achieved by the combination of two sets of measures:

- **Measure 1:** Subtract the combined "Basic Factor" percentage from the "Complex Factor" percentage to establish a net percentage. Rank all groups from highest to lowest overall positive (+) percentage. For example, if the "Early Career Stage" subgroup indicated 68 percent basic factors and 43 percent complex factors, their net percentage would be 25 percent.
- **Measure 2:** Survey non-volunteers on their future intent to volunteer and create a breakdown by subgroup. The percentage might be added to the net factor percentage above to create an overall score. A similar rating system might be created for individual non-volunteers as part of your association's volunteer prospecting system to aid in the recruitment process.

Turning Non-Volunteers into Volunteers

Conducting additional research related to why your members don't volunteer can take many forms and cover all the subject areas explored in Chapters 4–8. For example, if your findings on gender demographics show that either men or women are underrepresented in your volunteer ranks in comparison to your member demographics, you might consider reviewing your messages and strategies to ensure that both groups feel welcome.

Or considering tracking new volunteers for your organization versus those who have slipped away and then returned to the organization. Reflect on what you learn from this data and how you might encourage these members to stay involved by engaging them in different types of volunteer activities.

If you are part of the parent organization, are you fully aware of who is volunteering at the local level so that you aren't incorrectly labeling some members as non-volunteers?

Since we understand that some people are focused on volunteering close to home and therefore may say no to national positions, consider encouraging your chapters to send out a call for volunteers. Be sure to track the quality or follow-through on those promotions. Providing a template for chapters to use to make this easier for them is a great way to assist the chapters in recruitment efforts.

- Review Exhibit 9.2 and draft (or have a group of volunteers draft) a response for each of the 17 reasons provided for volunteering that highlights how your association does or provides that.

THE DECISION TO VOLUNTEER survey results suggest that volunteers do want to be rewarded or recognized and have voiced some options. Can you develop a system to capture feedback from your volunteers?

- Ask your volunteers (and members) about their professional values and then compare that to your organization's needs. Identify where there are gaps between the two.
- Is your volunteer selection clear on what professional experience and credentials are needed for certain positions? Have you audited this to ensure that it is still relevant?
- Direct (as opposed to passive) recruitment strategies appear to have better results. Ask your volunteers how they see your strategies and adjust them accordingly.

Study Design and Method

Participants

THE DECISION TO VOLUNTEER project was designed as a coalition of membership organizations to explore the reasons why people volunteer for career- and cause-related activities. Twenty-three organizations joined as cosponsors, shown on the following page.

Survey Planning and Implementation

We designed the survey during August–October 2007 using questions tested and validated in previous volunteerism studies, new questions germane to association volunteering, and questions used in our earlier study: THE DECISION TO JOIN (ASAE 2007). Each cosponsor identified a primary contact responsible as a liaison with ASAE & The Center. The primary contact was involved in the development of the questionnaire through consensus building during the project kick-off meeting held in Chicago on October 3, 2007 and in subsequent electronic communication. These liaisons also attended a post-survey meeting on February 29, 2008 in Washington, DC to discuss the results and discuss the most important findings.

The survey was deployed through an electronic survey service in waves beginning on November 7, 2007, and ending on December 31, 2007. The survey was customized for each cosponsor with their logo and custom questions, if any. All non-respondents received at least one follow-up communication.

Each cosponsor contributed between 5,000 and 10,000 member names, randomly selected, to this study. Most over-sampled their known volunteers, providing a maximum of 1,500 of their total sample in this category. Our analysis subsequently used weighted factors to account for this oversampling. The Internet survey was deployed to 185,975 individuals using the email address they provided as members. We received 26,305 responses for an

A Profile of the Cosponsors

The 23 cosponsoring organizations whose members participated in this survey vary considerably in their membership demographics. In eight of the cosponsoring organizations, women comprise less than 25 percent of the membership, and in five more organizations, men comprise less than 15 percent of the membership. Minority participation varies from 1 to 15 percent, and in four of the organizations, 25 to 50 percent of the members are outside of the United States.

With respect to their organizational characteristics, in 11 of the cosponsoring organizations, the parent is incorporated as a 501(c)(6) business league. Of the remainder, 10 are 501(c)(3) charities, and one is a 501(c)(4) social welfare organization. One-third were formed more than a century ago; five were organized post WWII.

In terms of their organizational complexity, all but one organization has chapters, branches, geographic groups, interest groups, or other components. Seven participating organizations have more than 150 components. In half of the organizations, components are part of the parent organization rather than independent affiliates. In most cases, members join the parent organization before electing to join chapters. In half of the organizations, national board members are directly elected by the membership.

While their missions vary, their activities are similar: Three quarters or more of the participating organizations are engaged in public advocacy, professional development and training, credentialing and certification, and in setting standards for their industry or profession.

Health Care, Occupational and Environmental Health
American Association of Orthodontists
American College of Healthcare Executives
American Heart Association National Center
American Industrial Hygiene Association
American Massage Therapy Association
American Nurses Association
American Society of Plastic Surgeons
American Speech-Language-Hearing Association
AORN Association of periOperative Registered Nurses
Oncology Nursing Society

Education
Illinois Education Association
National Association of Secondary School Principals
School Nutrition Association

Manufacturing and Engineering
American Society for Quality
American Society of Civil Engineers
American Society of Heating, Refrigerating and Air-Conditioning Engineers, Inc.
American Society of Mechanical Engineers
Institute of Electrical and Electronics Engineers
NACE International (Corrosion Engineers)
Society of Petroleum Engineers

Professional
American Institute of Certified Public Accountants
National Funeral Directors Association
Project Management Institute

overall response rate of 14 percent, ranging from a low of 9 percent to a high of 21 percent within each organization.

Weighting

Responses from the 26,305 respondents were weighted in the analysis to account for oversampling known volunteers. Weighting factors were calculated for each cosponsor based on the ratio of known volunteers to all members.

Questionnaire Design

The questionnaire covers three broad areas:

1. Volunteering in general
2. Volunteering for a cosponsor
3. Demographics

For purposes of this study, volunteering was specifically defined for respondents. This definition was adapted from a standard question used in the U.S. Bureau of Labor Statistic's Current Population Survey and elsewhere, as follows:

> *In this study, we are interested in all types of volunteering, not just the volunteer work you might do in your professional life, but also volunteering in your community, for schools, religious or any other types of organizations.*
>
> *The term "volunteer" for all questions in this survey refers to any activities for which people are not paid, except perhaps expenses. We want you to include only volunteer activities that you did through or for an organization, even if you did them only once in a while.*

With the goal of a comparative study in mind, we organized the Internet survey into three parts.

Part One

The first section of our survey addressed the general volunteering behavior of our respondents, all of whom are current members of one of the 23 cosponsoring organizations participating in this study. Eleven survey questions asked cosponsor members about whether, where, why, and how often they volunteered for any organization (including churches, charities, associations, or other organizations).

Part Two

We then asked a similar set of questions about the volunteer activity of members for the cosponsoring organization that submitted the name. We obtained the number of hours volunteered, how members first learned about volunteer opportunities offered by the cosponsor, and how satisfied volunteers are with their experiences.

Part Three

The third part of our survey captured demographic data about respondents, including their age, educational level, career level, employment status, gender, race, and family status. In national studies, many of these items are indicators of higher volunteering activity, including particularly educational level and family status.

Exact question and response wording, order, and response are shown in the Frequency Tables below.

Frequency Tables (Weighted)

Questionnaire Part One
Volunteering in General

Have you performed any work as a volunteer through or for any organization?

	Number: 20281
	%
In the last 12 months	77.1
In the past but not in the last 12 months	15.1
Never volunteered	7.8

I would start volunteering now if:

Asked only of people who have not volunteered in the last 12 months.
Mean shows the average rating on a 1–5 scale with 5=strongly agree. Shown in order with strongest agreement first.

	Number: 4636	
	Mean	Rank
I knew the volunteer opportunity was meaningful or made a difference in people's lives	4.29	1
I knew I had the skills needed to do a good job	4.06	2
The location was easily accessible to me	3.93	3
I was interested in volunteering	3.90	4
I did not lose income as a result	3.89	5
I could be given short-term assignments	3.77	6
I had more information about volunteer opportunities available to me	3.57	7
A volunteer organization would train me to do the work	3.54	8
My employer supported my participation as a volunteer	3.47	9
I knew it would make a difference to my profession or in my work	3.45	10
I was actually asked to volunteer	3.37	11
I knew someone else who also worked or volunteered there	3.34	12
I could volunteer electronically or virtually	3.32	13
I was recognized and appreciated for my work as a volunteer	3.31	14
I was not disappointed with volunteering in the past	3.29	15
The organization that needed help was one that had, in the past, helped me or someone I love	3.25	16
I was reimbursed for expenses such as meals or gas allowance	2.67	17

EXHIBIT A.3

Which of the following best describes the type(s) of organizations for which you volunteered in the last 12 months? (Check all that apply.)

Shown in order with the most frequently reported type of organization first.

Number: **16546**

	%	Rank
Civic, community service	47.7	1
Religious	45.1	2
Professional, technical, or trade	42.1	3
Educational or youth service	41.0	4
Sport, hobby, cultural, or arts	26.4	5
Nonprofit health organization other than hospital or clinic	14.7	6
Hospital or clinic	8.7	7
Environmental or animal care	6.5	8
Political group or party	5.4	9
Public safety	4.2	10

EXHIBIT A.4

Which of the following best describes the volunteer activities that you performed for organization(s) in the last 12 months? (Check all that apply.)

Shown in order with the most frequently reported volunteer activity first.

Number: **16546**

	%	Rank
Serving on board(s) or committee(s)	57.2	1
Direct service (e.g. preparing, serving, or delivering food, ushering, etc.)	44.4	2
Coach, referee, tutor, teacher, or mentor	40.5	3
Organizing groups and/or meetings	40.2	4
Fundraising or selling items to raise money	38.3	5
Working at a trade show, conference, or other meeting	17.1	6
Writing or presenting paper(s) or research reports at conferences or workshops	15.2	7
Setting professional or industry standards or providing technical input	14.6	8
Organizing promotional campaigns for events or other activities	13.6	9
Arts or creative activities	12.6	10
Providing counseling, medical care, fire/EMS, or protective services	11.8	11
Presenting or testifying on behalf of any organization to any legislative body (local, state, federal, or global advocacy)	5.2	12
Other	0.5	13

EXHIBIT A.5

Approximately how many total hours did you perform volunteer work for all the organizations you volunteered for in the last 12 months?

Number: **16546**

	%
1–12 hours	12.3
13–49 hours	28.3
50–99 hours	25.1
100–249 hours	22.1
250–499 hours	7.7
500 or more hours	4.6

For how many different organizations did you perform volunteer work in the last 12 months?

Number: **16546**

	%
One	18.8
Two	31.3
Three	28.3
Four	12.4
Five or more	9.1

When you volunteer, do you ever actively seek opportunities to contribute your workplace skills?

Number: **16546**

	%
Yes	72.1
No	27.9

What effect do you think volunteering has had on your career, or if you are self employed, on your business?

Number: **16546**

	%
Very negative	0.1
2	0.8
3	13.7
4	26.5
Very positive	48.3
Do not know	10.7
Mean rating (do not know excluded):	**4.37**

Regardless of your previous volunteer experience, how important or accurate would the following statements be for you in doing volunteer work?

This table compares volunteers according to what they believe they gain through volunteer work. Mean shows the average rating on a 1–5 scale with 5=very important. The 15 questions asked of all respondents are displayed in rows, grouped according to the six underlying dimensions identified in the Volunteer Functions Inventory (See bibliography: Clary, Snyder, and Stukas 1996). See also exhibit A.17 to compare respondent's attitudes toward volunteering for the cosponsor.

Number: **20281**

	Mean	VFI Dimension
I feel it is important to help others	4.38	
I can do something for a profession or cause that is important to me	4.12	Values
I feel compassion toward people in need	4.08	
Volunteering allows me to gain a new perspective on things	3.88	
I can explore my own strengths	3.41	Understanding
I can learn new skills through direct, hands-on experience	3.37	
Volunteering makes me feel needed	3.17	
Volunteering brings me satisfaction or recognition that I do not get at work	3.12	Enhancement
I can make new contacts that might help my business or career	2.70	
Volunteer experience looks good on my resume	2.37	
Volunteering helps me to explore different career options	2.23	Career
Volunteering gives a competitive advantage to my business	2.18	
Volunteering can help me get my foot in the door at a place where I would like to work	2.02	
Volunteering is important to the people I respect	3.30	Social
Volunteering helps me deal with some of my own problems	2.29	Protective

Questionnaire Part Two
Volunteering for a Cosponsor

In the last 12 months, have you done any of the following as a volunteer (in person, online, or in any other way) on behalf of [cosponsor]?
Shown in order with the most frequently reported cosponsor volunteer activity first.

Number: **20281**

	%	Rank
Provided mentoring, coaching, or tutoring for members, students, or others	14.3	1
Provided professional advice	13.3	2
Recruited a member or members	12.4	3
Served on a committee for a local chapter or section	10.9	4
Spoke or presented a paper	8.8	5
Participated in a discussion group, expert panel, or report	8.7	6
Served on the board for a local chapter or section	7.3	7
Moderated or facilitated discussion groups at meetings or elsewhere	6.4	8
Raised funds	6.0	9
Reviewed a paper or proposal for a publication	5.7	10
Submitted a paper or manuscript for publication	5.0	11
Served on a committee for the parent organization	4.6	12
Served on a technical committee or reviewed standards and practices	4.5	13
Reviewed proposals for conferences or projects	4.5	14
Reviewed research, conducted literature review or resource reviews, or analyzed data	4.2	15
Reviewed applications as part of accreditation, certification or competitive program	3.2	16
Wrote proposals, grant applications or business plans	2.8	17
Made a presentation or testified on behalf of the organization to any legislative body (local, state, national or global advocacy)	2.3	18
Served on the board for the parent organization	1.6	19
Prepared background for regulators, the press, or others	1.5	20

Which of the following best describes why you do not currently volunteer for [cosponsor] now? If more than one, select up to five.
Asked only of those who did not check any activity described in Exhibit A.10 above. Shown in order with the most frequently reported reason first.

Number: **12903**

	%	Rank
I do not have enough information about volunteer opportunities available to me	38.7	1
I volunteer elsewhere	35.1	2
They never asked me to volunteer	28.7	3
I do not know of any volunteer opportunities that can be done electronically or virtually	23.0	4
I do not know of any short-term assignments for volunteers	22.4	5
The location is inconvenient for me	16.3	6
I do not know anyone who works or volunteers for them	15.0	7
I am not interested in volunteering for them	11.5	8
My employer does not support it	5.0	9
I do not think volunteering for them would make a difference in my profession or work	4.9	10
I am concerned about losing income as a result	4.8	11
I do not have the training necessary to volunteer for them	4.3	12
I do not have the skills needed to do a good job	3.4	13
They do not reimburse volunteers for expenses like travel or meals	2.6	14
I have been disappointed when volunteering for them in the past	1.6	15
They do not offer enough opportunities for volunteers to network with one another	1.5	16
They didn't accept my offer to volunteer	1.4	17
Term limits or other policy adopted by the organization prevents me from volunteering now	0.8	18
They do not recognize and appreciate the work of volunteers	0.6	19
Volunteering is not supported in my country	0.6	20
Other (mainly "no time" with no other reason given)	11.9	

Have you ever volunteered for [cosponsor] in the past?

Asked only of those who did not check any activity described in Exhibit A.10 above.

Number: 20281

	%
Yes	8.7
No	54.9
Not asked, respondent volunteered in the past 12 months	36.4

EXHIBIT A.13

How long ago was that?

Asked only of those who answered 'yes' to the question shown in Exhibit A.12 above.

Number: 1758

	%
1–2 years ago	13.5
3–5 years ago	28.1
5–10 years ago	30.2
More than 10 years ago	28.2

EXHIBIT A.14

On average, how many hours did you perform volunteer work for [cosponsor] in the last 12 months?

Asked only of those who checked one or more of the activities described in Exhibit A.10 above.

Number: 7380

	%
1–12 hours	57.2
13–49 hours	26.5
50–99 hours	10.2
100–249 hours	4.4
250–499 hours	1.2
500 or more hours	0.6

EXHIBIT A.15

Have you performed any volunter work for [cosponsor] by "virtual volunteering," e.g. volunteer activities that are completed, in whole or in part, via the Internet on a home, work, or public access computer?

*Asked only of those who either checked one or more of the activities described in Exhibit A.10 **or** answered "yes' to the question shown in Exhibit A.12 above.*

Number: 9153

	%
Yes	18.8
No	81.2

EXHIBIT A.16

How did you first learn about the volunteer opportunities available to you through [cosponsor]? Please select only one.

*Asked only of those who either checked one or more of the activities described in Exhibit A.10 **or** answered "yes" to the question shown in Exhibit A.12 above. Shown in order with most frequent response first.*

Number: 9153

	%	Rank
I don't recall	26.6	1
Through a local chapter or section	14.2	2
At a meeting, conference, or other event	13.4	3
I was asked by another volunteer	13.3	4
A staff member of the organization asked me to volunteer	8.9	5
I answered a call/ad for volunteers	5.1	6
Through my employer (current or past)	5.1	7
Through a professor or someone at my university or school	3.7	8
Through a posting on their web site	3.0	9
I contacted the organization and offered to volunteer	2.8	10
I saw an advertisement in the organization's magazine or other publication	2.3	11
Other	1.6	

How important are each of the following reasons to you in doing volunteer work for [cosponsor]?

This table compares volunteers according to what they believe they gain through volunteer work
for the cosponsor. *Mean shows the average rating on a 1–5 scale with 5=very important. The 15 questions asked of all respondents who currently volunteer for the cosponor (see Exhibit A.10) OR who have volunteered for the cosponsor anytime in the past (see Exhibit A.12). Items are grouped according to the six underlying dimensions identified in the Volunteer Functions Inventory (See bibliography: Clary, Snyder, and Stukas 1996). See also Exhibit A.9 to compare volunteering for the cosponsor with respondent's attitudes toward volunteer work in general.*

	Number:	9153	
		Mean	**VFI Dimension**
I feel it is important to help others		3.89	
I can do something for a profession or cause that is important to me		3.94	Values
I feel compassion toward people in need		3.52	
Volunteering allows me to gain a new perspective on things		3.41	
I can explore my own strengths		3.24	Understanding
I can learn new skills through direct, hands-on experience		3.24	
Volunteering makes me feel needed		2.73	
Volunteering brings me satisfaction or recognition that I do not get at work		2.67	Enhancement
I can make new contacts that might help my business or career		2.89	
Volunteer experience looks good on my resume		2.50	
Volunteering helps me to explore different career options		2.37	Career
Volunteering gives me a competitive advantage to my business		2.41	
Volunteering can help get my foot in the door at a place where I would like to work		2.22	
Volunteering is important to the people I respect		3.09	Social
Volunteering helps me deal with some of my own problems		2.08	Protective

How satisfied are you with the following aspects of your volunteer experience with [cosponsor]?

Asked only of those who either checked one or more of the activities described in Exhibit A.10 ***or*** *answered "yes' to the question shown in Exhibit A.12 above.*
Mean shows the average rating on a 1–5 scale with 5=very satisfied. Shown in order with highest satisfaction first.

	Number:	9153	
		Mean	**Rank**
Helping you feel that you are giving back to your profession		3.86	1
Having opportunities to meet, work, and socialize with others in your field or profession		3.83	2
Working with others toward a common goal		3.78	3
Using your existing skills		3.74	4
Feeling respected, appreciated, and valued		3.59	5
Opportunity to take a leadership role		3.58	6
Ability to make choices about when you volunteer		3.54	7
Helping you connect with the mission of the organization		3.52	8
Ability to make choices about what you do as a volunteer		3.51	9
Learning new skills		3.45	10
Receiving feedback about your performance		3.20	11
Receiving training needed to be effective		3.18	12
Receiving incentives like stipends, transportation, and/or meals		2.82	13

EXHIBIT A.19

Please use the scale provided below to rate your overall satisfaction with volunteering for [cosponsor].

*Asked only of those who either checked one or more of the activities described in Exhibit A.10 **or** answered "yes' to the question shown in Exhibit A.12 above.*

	Number: 9153
	%
Very dissatisfied	1.5
2	5.8
3	31.5
4	31.5
Very satisfied	16.3
No response	13.4
Mean (no response excluded)	**3.64**

EXHIBIT A.20

How likely is it that you will be a volunteer for [cosponsor] within the next 12 months?

Asked of all respondents.

	Number: 20281
	%
Very unlikely	27.1
2	20.6
3	24.6
4	11.7
Very likely	13.0
No response	3.0
Mean (no response excluded)	**2.62**

EXHIBIT A.21

How likely is it that you would recommend volunteering for [cosponsor] to a friend or colleague?

Asked of all respondents.

	Number: 20281
	%
Very unlikely	18.7
2	17.5
3	29.6
4	16.9
Very likely	13.3
No response	4.0
Mean (no response excluded)	**2.88**

Questionnaire Part Three
Demographics
(Asked of all respondents unless otherwise noted)

EXHIBIT A.22

Which of the following best describes your current employment situation?

	Number: 20281
	%
Employed full time (35 or more hours per week)	88.9
Employed part time (less than 35 hours per week)	6.6
Currently a full time student, unemployed, or between jobs	1.6
Retired	2.8

EXHIBIT A.23

Which of the following best describes the type of organization in which you are employed?
Asked only if employed full- or part-time (See Exhibit A.22).

	Number: 19381
	%
Private sector	49.7
Academia/educational institution/school	19.5
Nonprofit organization	10.8
Government	7.0
Self-employed or solo practice	13.0

EXHIBIT A.24

Which best describes your current career situation?
*Asked only if employed full or part time (See Exhibit A.22) **and** excludes academia, unemployed, self-employed, and retired (See Exhibit A.23).*

	Number: 12342
	%
Entry level	6.3
Mid level	53.6
Senior level but not chief executive	31.8
Chief executive	8.3

EXHIBIT A.25

What year did you begin working in the profession or industry in which you are now employed?
Asked only if employed full or part time (See Exhibit A.22).

	Number: 19381
	%
Before 1980	24.0
1980–1989	29.8
1990–1999	26.5
2000 or later	19.7
Mean year	**1988**

EXHIBIT A.26

Which of the following best describes your highest level of education?

	Number: 20281
	%
High school or less	2.8
Some college	5.9
Associate degree or equivalent	7.7
Bachelor's degree or equivalent	31.2
Master's degree or equivalent	33.8
PhD, JD, EdD, or equivalent	8.8
MD or DDS	9.8

EXHIBIT A.27

What is your gender?

	Number: 20281
	%
Male	56.6
Female	43.4

What year were you born? (classified)

	Number: **20281**
	%
Pre-war (1945 or before)	8.7
Early Boom (1946–1954)	25.9
Late Boom (1955–1962)	29.6
Gen X (1963–1976)	29.5
Millennials (1977 or later)	6.3
Mean year	**1959**

Does at least one other member of your immediate family (parents, siblings, spouse, or children) currently engage in volunteer activity or have they done so in the past?

	Number: **20281**
	%
Yes	79.1
No	19.0
Not applicable/No immediate family members	1.9

Which best describes your marital/partner status?

	Number: **20281**
	%
Married or partnered	84.1
Unmarried or not partnered	15.9

Do you have children under 18 years old living in your household?

	Number: **20281**
	%
Yes, full time	41.8
Yes, part of the time	1.9
No	56.2

Responses by Region (Map)

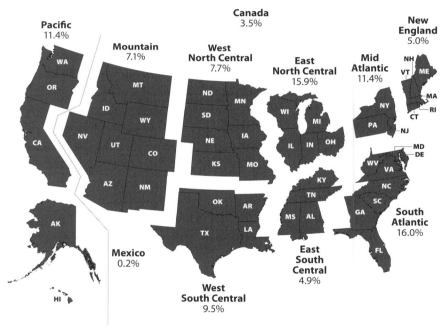

Pacific 11.4%

Canada 3.5%

New England 5.0%

Mountain 7.1%

West North Central 7.7%

East North Central 15.9%

Mid Atlantic 11.4%

South Atlantic 16.0%

Mexico 0.2%

East South Central 4.9%

West South Central 9.5%

Military or U.S. Territories 0.3%

Outside North America 7.1%

Region

	Number: 20281
	%
New England	5.0
Mid Atlantic	11.4
South Atlantic	16.0
East North Central	15.9
East South Central	4.9
West North Central	7.7
West South Central	9.5
Mountain	7.1
Pacific	11.4
Military or U.S. Territories	0.3
Canada	3.5
Mexico	0.2
Outside North America	7.1

EXHIBIT A.34

World Location

	Number: 20281
	%
United States	89.2
Canada and Mexico	3.7
Outside North America	7.1

EXHIBIT A.35

Race (U.S. respondents only)

	Number: 20281
	%
American Indian/Alaska Native	0.7
Asian	4.9
Black or African-American	2.7
Hispanic	2.6
Native Hawaiian/Pacific Islander	0.2
White	74.5
More than one race	1.2
No answer or not asked	13.1

The Decision to Volunteer 2008 Bibliography

Allison, Lora D., Morris A. Okun, and Kathy S. Dutridge. 2002. Assessing volunteer motives: a comparison of open-ended probe and likert rating scales. *Journal of Community and Applied Social Psychology*, 12: 243–55.

Brudney, Jeffrey L. 1990. *Fostering volunteer programs in the public sector: Planning, initiating, and managing voluntary activities*. San Francisco: Jossey-Bass.

———. 2005. Designing and managing volunteer programs. In *The Jossey-Bass handbook of nonprofit leadership and management, 2nd ed.,* ed. Robert D. Herman and Associates, 310–44. San Francisco: Jossey-Bass.

———, and Beth Gazley. 2006. Moving ahead or falling behind? Volunteer promotion and data collection. *Nonprofit Management and Leadership*, 16(3): 259–76.

Bureau of Labor Statistics. 2004. *Volunteering in the United States: A supplement to the September 2004 Current Population Survey.* http://stats.bls.gov/news.release/archives/volun_12162004.pdf

———. 2008. *Volunteering in the United States 2007.* http://www.bls.gov/news.release/volun.toc.htm

Burns, David J., Jane Reid, Mark Toncar, Cynthia Anderson, and Cassandra Wells. 2008. The effect of gender on the motivation of members of Generation Y college students to volunteer. *Journal of Nonprofit and Public Sector Marketing* 19(1): 99–118.

Center for Health Communication, Harvard School of Public Health. 2004. *Reinventing aging: Baby Boomers and civic engagement.* Boston: Harvard College. http://assets.aarp.org/rgcenter/general/boomers_engagement.pdf

Center on Philanthropy at Indiana University. 2007. *Giving USA.* Indianapolis, IN: Center on Philanthropy.

———. 2008. *Generational differences in charitable giving and in motivations for giving: A report prepared for Campbell & Company.* Indianapolis, IN: Center on Philanthropy.

Clary, E. Gil, and Mark Snyder. 1999. The motivations to volunteer: Theoretical and practical considerations. *Current Directions in Psychological Science* 8(5): 156–9.

———, Mark Snyder, Robert D. Ridge, John Copeland, Arthur A. Stukas, Julie Haugen, and Peter Miene. 1998. Understanding and assessing the motivations of volunteers: A functional approach. *Journal of Personality and Social Psychology* 74(6): 1516–30.

———, Mark Snyder, and Arthur A. Stukas. 1996. Volunteers' motivations: findings from a national survey. *Nonprofit and Voluntary Sector Quarterly* 25(4): 485–505.

Cnaan, Ram A., and Robin S. Goldberg-Glen. 1991. Measuring motivation to volunteer in human services. *Journal of Applied Behavioral Science* 27(3): 269–84.

Corporation for National and Community Service. 2007. *Issue brief: volunteer retention.* Washington, DC: Corporation for National and Community Service. http://www.nationalservice.org/pdf/VIA/VIA_brief_retention.pdf

———. 2008. *Effective use of volunteers by nonprofits and congregations.* Washington, DC: Corporation for National and Community Service. http://www.nationalservice.org/about/volunteering/nonprofit.asp

Cufaude, Jeffrey. 2000. Cultivating new leadership. *Association Management:* 73–8.

Dalton, James and Monica Dignam. 2007. *The decision to join: How individuals determine value and why they choose to belong.* Washington, DC: ASAE and the Center for Association Leadership.

Deloitte LLP. 2008. *2008 Deloitte Volunteer Impact Survey.* http://www.deloitte.com/dtt/article/0,1002,sid%253D2255%2526cid%253D203301,00.html

Eisner, David. 2005. *Building democracy through service.* Berkeley, CA: PACE: Philanthropy for Active Civic Engagement. http://www.pacefunders.org/pdf/essays/Eisner%20FINAL.pdf

Ellis, Susan J. 1996. *From the top down: The executive role in volunteer program success.* Philadelphia: Energize, Inc.

———, and Katherine H. Campbell. 2005. *By the people: A history of Americans as volunteers.* Philadelphia: Energize, Inc.

Esmond, Judy, and Patrick Dunlop. 2004. *Developing the volunteer motivation inventory to assess the underlying motivational drives of volunteers in Western Australia.* Inglewood, WA, Australia: CLAN WA, Inc. http://www.mtd4u.com/resources/MotivationFinalReport.pdf

Farmer, Steven M., and Donald B. Fedor. 1999. Volunteer participation and withdrawal: A psychological contract perspective on the role of expectations and organizational support. *Nonprofit Management and Leadership* 9(4): 349–67.

Fletcher, Thomas D., and Debra Major. 2004. Medical students' motivations to volunteer: an examination of the nature of gender differences. *Sex Roles* 109–14.

Gazley, Beth. 2008. Personnel recruitment and retention in the nonprofit sector. In *Public personnel administration: Problems and prospects, 5th ed.,* ed. Steven W. Hays, Richard C. Kearney, and Jerrold Coggburn. Upper Saddle River, NJ: Prentice-Hall.

Greenslade, Jaimi H., and Katherine M. White. 2005. The prediction of above-average participation in volunteerism: A test of the theory of planned behavior and the volunteers functions inventory in older Australian adults. *Journal of Social Psychology* 145(2): 155–72.

Grimm, Robert Jr., Kevin Cramer, Nathan Dietz, LaMonica Shelton, Lillian Dote, Carla Manuel, and Shelby Jennings. 2007. *Volunteering in America: 2007 state trends and rankings in civic life.* Washington, DC: Corporation for National and Community Service. http://www.nationalservice.gov/about/volunteering/states.asp

Hager, Mark, and Jeffrey L. Brudney. 2004. *Volunteer management practices and retention of volunteers.* Washington, DC: The Urban Institute.

Houle, Barbara J., Brad J. Sagarin, and Martin F. Kaplan. 2005. A functional approach to volunteerism: Do volunteer motives predict task preference? *Basic and Applied Social Psychology,* 27(4): 337–44.

Independent Sector. 2003. *Experience at work: Volunteering and giving among Americans 50 and over.* Washington, DC: Independent Sector.

Jamison, Irma B. 2003. Turnover and retention among volunteers in human services agencies. *Review of Public Personnel Administration,* 23(2): 114–32.

Kirsch, Arthur D., Keith M. Hume, and Nadine T. Jalandoni. 2000. *Giving and volunteering in the United States: Findings from a national survey, 1999 ed.* Washington, DC: Independent Sector.

Knoke, David, and Randall Thomson. 1977. Voluntary association membership trends and the family life cycle. *Social Forces* 56: 48–65.

Kutner, Gail, and Jeffrey Love. 2003. *Time and money: an in-depth look at 45+ volunteers and donors: findings from a multicultural survey of Americans 45 and older.* Washington, DC: American Association of Retired Persons.

Leete, Laura. 2006. Work in the nonprofit sector. In *The nonprofit sector: A research handbook, 2nd ed,* ed. Walter W. Powell and Richard Steinberg, 159–79. New Haven: Yale University Press.

Lindblom, Dawn. 2001. *Baby boomers and the new age of volunteerism.* Washington, DC: Corporation for National and Community Service.

Macduff, Nancy. 2005. Societal changes and the rise of the episodic volunteer. In *Emerging Areas of Volunteering,* ed. Jeffrey L. Brudney, 1(2): 49–61. Indianapolis, IN: ARNOVA.

McCurley, Steve, and Rick Lynch. 1996. *Volunteer management: Mobilizing all the resources of the community.* Downers Grove, IL: Heritage Arts Publishing.

Murray, Vic, and Yvonne Harrison. 2005. Virtual volunteering. In *Emerging areas of volunteering,* ed. Jeffrey L. Brudney, 1(2): 31–48. Indianapolis, IN: ARNOVA.

National Council of Nonprofit Associations. 2006. *The United States nonprofit sector.* Washington, DC: NCNA.

Okun, Morris A., Alicia Barr, and A. Regula Herzog. 1998. Motivation to volunteer by older adults: A test of competing measurement models. *Psychology and Aging* 13(4): 608–21.

Omoto, Allen M., Mark Snyder, and Steven C. Martino. 2000. Volunteerism and the life course: Investigating age-related agendas for action. *Basic and Applied Social Psychology* 22(3): 191–7.

Papadakis, Katerina, Tonya Griffin, and Joel Frater. 2004. Understanding volunteers' motivations. *Proceedings of the 2004 Northeastern Recreation Research Symposium,* 321–6.

Peterson, Dane K. 2004. Recruitment strategies for encouraging participation in corporate volunteer programs. *Journal of Business Ethics* 49: 371–86.

Prisuta, Robert H. 2003. *What can the attitudes and actions of Boomers today tell us about their future role as volunteers?* Presentation to the Harvard School of Public Health–MetLife Foundation Conference on Baby Boomers and Retirement: Impact on Civic Engagement, Cambridge, MA, October 9.

Putnam, Robert D. 2000. *Bowling alone: The collapse and revival of American community.* New York: Simon & Schuster.

Rotolo, Thomas, and John Wilson. 2007. Sex segregation in volunteer work. *The Sociological Quarterly,* 48: 559–85.

———, and John Wilson. 2006. Employment sector and volunteering: The contribution of nonprofit and public sector workers to the volunteer labor force. *The Sociological Quarterly* 47: 21–40.

Rousseau, Denise M. 1995. *Psychological contracts in organizations.* Thousand Oaks, CA: Sage.

Smith, Justin D., Angela Ellis, and Georgina Brewis. 2005. Cross-national volunteering: A developing movement? In *Emerging areas of volunteering,* ed. Jeffrey L. Brudney, 1(2): 63–75. Indianapolis, IN: ARNOVA.

Tang, Fengyan. 2006. What resources are needed for volunteerism? A life course perspective. *The Journal of Applied Gerontology* 25(5): 375–90.

Toppe, Christopher. M., Arthur. D. Kirsch, and Jocabel Michel. 2002. *Giving and volunteering in the United States 2001: Findings from a national survey.* Washington, DC: Independent Sector.

Tschirhart, Mary. 2005. Employee volunteer programs. In *Emerging areas of volunteering,* ed. Jeffrey L. Brudney, 1(2): 13–29. Indianapolis, IN: ARNOVA.

Weitzman, Murray S., Nadine T. Jalandoni, Linda M. Lampkin, and Thomas H. Pollak. 2002. *The new nonprofit almanac and desk reference.* New York: John Wiley and Sons.

Wilson, John. 2000. Volunteering. *Annual Review of Sociology* 26: 215–40.

———, and Marc Musick. 1997. Who cares? Toward an integrated theory of volunteering. *American Sociological Review* 62: 694–713.

Index

age impact on, 44–45, 54, 55
assessing, 24, 37
association members, 34
employment connection to, 73, 74, 83
engagement patterns emerging from, 27
gender impact on, 70
geographic differences in, 97
motivation impact on, 13
volunteer rate differences due to, 41–42
Pre-school children's parents as volunteers, 58
Private sector, volunteers from, 28, 74, 76, 80, 82, 83, 88
Professional advice, volunteers as source of, 28, 78
Professional benefits of volunteering, 3, 12, 24, 32, 34, 46, 97
Professional development of volunteers, 12
Professional organizations, volunteering for, 8, 10, 19, 34
Professional responsibilities, impact on volunteer capacity, 2, 54, 99
Professionals, mentoring and support for, volunteer role in, 1
Professional service, volunteer, 8, 18, 44, 46
Professional volunteering. *See also* Career-related volunteering
    alternatives to, 108
    broader context of, 2
    employer support for, 74
    employment sector breakdown for, 75–76, 82
    family status impact on, 60, 61, 67, 67t, 70
    gender differences in, 59
    geographic breakdown for, 91, 93
    opportunities, importance of, 45
    parental status and, 67
    post-retirement, 54, 56
    research on, 1
    retirement from, 36
    satisfaction with, 22
    values as motive behind, 2–3
    workplace volunteering, 1, 2, 9, 83–84
    of younger persons, 53
Professions
    volunteer motivations, differing for, 10
    volunteer work paralleling, 4
    volunteer work related to, 9
Psychological contract, 11, 13
Public health, volunteer role in improving, 6
Public safety volunteering, 59, 60–61
Public sector, volunteers from, 84

Q

Quality of life, volunteer role in improving, 6, 10
Quitting volunteer activity, reasons for, 11, 36, 99–100

R

Racial composition of volunteers, 8, 15–16, 16f, 53
Rates of volunteering, 7, 8–9, 30, 60, 62t, 76t, 90t
Recognition of volunteers
    age and career level impact on, 42
    employee recruitment through, 84, 85
    examining, 25
    expectation of, 11, 24
    gender and, 68
    incorporation of, statistics on, 12
    informal/ad hoc volunteering, 3, 6, 24, 30, 37
    lack, consequences of, 107
    level of affiliation as factor in, 27
    requirements for, 109
Recommendations from volunteers
    age differences in, 51, 52, 52t
    employment sector breakdown for, 69t, 80, 81t
    gender differences in, 69t
    geographic differences in, 96t
    likelihood of, 22, 22t, 24
    recruitment, factor in, 21
Record keeping on volunteers, 12
Recruitment as volunteer activity
    ad hoc nature of, 46
    age breakdown for, 53
    employment sector breakdown for, 78
    encouraging, 39
    gender breakdown for, 68
    importance of, 30
    long-distance, 104
    volunteer category breakdown for, 28
Recruitment of volunteers
    active versus passive, 3, 104–105
    age, relationship to, 42, 50t, 53, 54, 55, 56
    challenges, 19–20
    community volunteering, 1
    employment sector breakdown for, 83
    factors in effective, 11
    gender differences in, 68, 68t, 69, 70, 110
    geographic differences in, 93, 95t, 97, 104
    importance of, 5, 21, 52
    incomplete, impact of, 10, 102

information gathering concerning, 14
international, 91, 96
level of affiliation as factor in, 27
methods and strategies for, 3, 15, 24, 32, 54, 74, 76, 84, 104, 105, 110
minorities, 8
opportunities, 19–20
surveys covering, 14
volunteer type, breakdown by, 31–32, 31t
from workplace, 9
young volunteers, 9, 51
Reliance on volunteers, consequences of heavy, 34, 107
Religious endeavors, volunteering related to, 59, 61
Religious organizations, volunteering for, 8
Research, volunteer involvement in, 83
Responsibilities, balancing volunteering with other, 100, 104
Responsibility, volunteer level of, 28
Retention of volunteers
    challenges to, 9, 11
    factors in effective, 12
    importance of effective, 5
    methods and strategies for, 3, 15, 24, 54
    probing future, 22t
Retirees as volunteers, 17, 54, 56
Retirement impact on volunteering, 36, 51–52, 53, 54, 55

S

Satisfaction with volunteering
    age and career level impact on, 42, 51–52, 51t, 55, 55–56
    association volunteering, 21–22
    employment sector breakdown for, 80–82, 80t, 81t
    factors affecting, 27
    gender impact on, 68, 69t
    geographic differences in, 95, 95t, 97
    overview, 21t, 22t
    volunteer category breakdown, 34–36, 34t, 37t, 39
School-age children's parents as volunteers, 58
Scouting, volunteering in, 8
Screening procedures for volunteers, 12
Self-employed persons as non-volunteers, 102
Self-employed persons as volunteers, 17, 17f, 28, 74, 75–76, 80, 82, 83, 84, 85, 89
Self-improvement, 42
Self-serving motives for volunteering, 34

Service, direct
    age impact on preference for, 44
    gender impact on preference for, 59
    as volunteering motive, 42
Shapers (volunteer category), 28, 28f, 30, 31, 32, 34, 35, 36, 38, 39, 106
Short-term volunteering, 9, 11, 102, 104
Skills
    contributing, 46t, 55, 82, 91, 91t, 116t
    learning and enhancing, 34, 45, 82, 85, 91, 109
    non-volunteer concern about having, 100, 102, 104, 106
Social motivation for volunteering, 32, 34, 42
Social needs, volunteer role in meeting, 6, 23t, 24
Social pressure for volunteering, 10
Social/professional network, volunteering role in developing, 82, 109
Social relationships, strengthening, 13
Social welfare organizations, volunteering for, 6
Socioeconomic status impact on volunteering, 7, 8, 12, 23, 83, 87, 104
Sports and hobby volunteering, 8, 59, 61. *See also* Coaching
Staff *versus* volunteer turnover, 11
Staff-volunteer relations
    acceptance problems, 11
    communication, 2
    maintaining and improving, 106, 109
    staff training in work with volunteers, 12, 25
Stipends for volunteers, 37
Survey methods, 14

T

Tasks
    matching volunteers to, 12, 24, 32
    preferences, motivation impact on, 13
    variation in, 54
Tax deductions for volunteer expense reimbursement, 105–106
Teachers (volunteer category), 28, 28f, 30, 31, 35, 38, 39, 58
Team-based volunteering, 84
Technical and trade volunteering, 59, 60
Teenagers as volunteers, 8
Telecommunications devices and volunteering, 70
Time
    commitment capacity, 39, 58, 99

About the Authors

Beth Gazley is assistant professor in the School of Public and Environmental Affairs (SPEA) at Indiana University-Bloomington, where she teaches non-profit and public management. She has conducted research and published on civic engagement and volunteer management, government-nonprofit relations and inter-organizational collaboration, the role of nonprofits in emergency planning, nonprofit management capacity, and other topics related to civil society and new governance. She has published in *Public Administration Review, Nonprofit and Voluntary Sector Quarterly, Nonprofit Management and Leadership, Big Ideas in Collaborative Public Management* (M.E Sharpe, 2008), and elsewhere. Professor Gazley has received recognition from the Academy of Management and ARNOVA for her research, and was a 2007 recipient of a Trustee Teaching Award. Before entering academia, Professor Gazley served for 15 years in public interest politics and the nonprofit sector as an association manager, fundraiser and management consultant. She resides in Bloomington, Indiana.

Monica Dignam is vice president, industry and market research, at ASAE & The Center for Association Leadership. She has been a professional researcher for more than 30 years. Before coming to ASAE & The Center in 2004, Dignam was president of Monalco, Inc., a Milwaukee firm specializing in research for associations. She was also an active volunteer, serving on the ASAE Marketing Section Council and contributing as both a writer and as a speaker to ASAE & The Center and a number of allied societies of association executives. Dignam is a past board member of Professional Dimensions, a Milwaukee professional women's group, and a founding member of the Washington area's Women in Advertising and Marketing. She is also a member of the Qualitative Research Consultants Association and the Association for Research on Nonprofit Organizations and Voluntary Action.